GW00393285

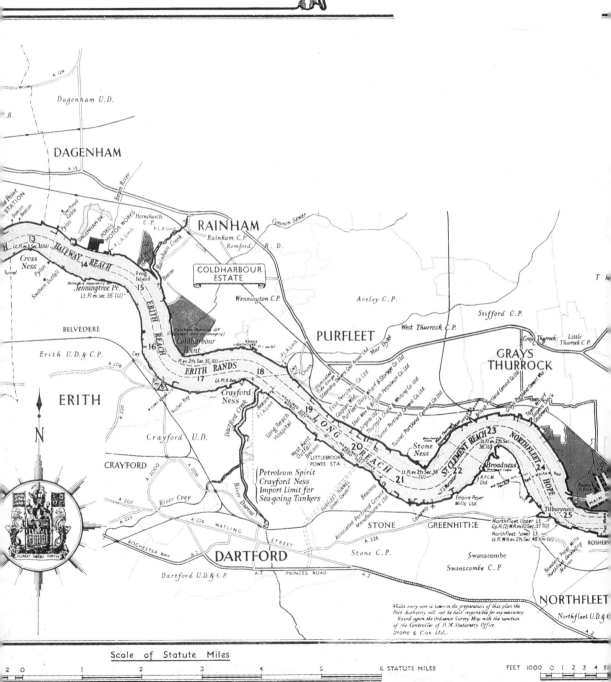

Whilst every care is taken in the preparation of this plan the Port Authority will not be held responsible for any inaccuracy. Based upon the Ordnance Survey Map with the sanction of the Controller of H.M. Stationery Office. Stone & Cox Ltd.

Scale of Statute Miles

FEET 1000

THAMES CAVALCADE

Overleaf: *Busy shipping scene in the Royal Albert Dock, 1965, with the* Samaria *under tow and the quays lined with deep-sea cargo vessels from all over the world.*

THAMES CAVALCADE

The heyday of the Haven

L. M. BATES

TERENCE DALTON LIMITED
LAVENHAM, SUFFOLK 1991

Published by
TERENCE DALTON LIMITED
ISBN 0 86138 090 8
© L. M. Bates, 1991

Text photoset in 10/11 pt Baskerville
Printed in Great Britain at
The Lavenham Press Limited, Lavenham, Suffolk

Contents

Acknowledgements

MY WARMEST thanks go to Thames-side libraries and other institutions which over the last three or four decades have given me scholarly judgements on much that I have picked up along the river. My gratitude also goes to Miss Dorothy Tomlinson for permission to quote extensively from the work of her late father, H. M. Tomlinson, to Mr R. R. Aspinal, BA, of the Museum in Dockland for helping to chart my course through the maze of modern dockland development, and to Mr Harry Green for making available to me some of the invaluable electronic gadgetry of his office.

It is several years since I retired from active Thames life and it has been only with the help of these and a host of other kind friends that I have been able to keep afloat in a vast sea of change. I have been pestering these Thames-siders—scores of individuals as well as official bodies such as the Port of London Authority, Trinity House, Docklands Development Corporation, Thames Water, the National Rivers Authority and the Cutty Sark Maritime Trust—for information and pictures, but, warmly grateful, I should need a supplement to mention all the individual names involved. I must, however, record personal thanks to friends who have taken or have caused to be taken photographs not otherwise available—Roger Mutton of the PLA, Norman Silveston of the Sheerness Camera Club, Peter Hamon of Job Box, Paul Brown and Norman Pennington of Gosfield Hall. I am also grateful to the Wapping Group of Artists for providing the humorous drawings illustrating their activities. Pictures reproduced by courtesy of the Museum in Dockland are from the Museum's Docklands Project, PLA Collection.

Finally, I am very grateful to Mr James Moore, who has shaped the ends of some rough-hewn paragraphs.

Introduction

AMONG the world's great rivers the Thames is geographically insignificant, but for centuries it has been great by almost any other measure, whether as a harbour for famous ships, a seat of world commerce or a stage for national pageantry. During its long story it has been the setting for a cavalcade of incomparable individualists and a backcloth for events which inspired or reflected changes in the fortunes of English-speaking peoples.

To ride the tide down river is now, for some of us, a sad and nostalgic pilgrimage, for the abandoned docks, derelict wharves, rusting cranes and absence of shipping all say *sic transit*. And even if the new houses and flats rising from these ashes of industry eventually embellish a river of pleasure with its own folk lore, much will have been lost. Beneath the steel and concrete of the new development lies a great wealth of tradition; a force to be reckoned with, for a present which ignores the past gravely imperils the future.

The Port of London, once prospering between the sea and Teddington, a distance of some seventy miles, has shrunk to a concentration of berths and cargo-handling gear at Tilbury Docks in Essex and a few privately owned riverside wharves able to meet modern challenges. All this has been brought about by bigger ships and space-demanding containers, neither of which could be handled at the old established upriver docks and wharves. Nevertheless, the importance and efficiency of the new port at Tilbury must not be undervalued: it is still the largest British port and one of the world's major sea terminals.

But it is the changes that I write about; of men I knew, now nearly all dead; of beautiful ships, nearly all gone; of the old ramshackle riverside, now greatly changed; of churches in which few now worship; of yarns in old round bellied pubs about events mostly forgotten.

In a way this book is a tying together of loose ends. I have been writing about the tidal Thames for half a century and it is impossible within the limits of time and space to avoid occasionally treading some paths again. But all those earlier records were disjointed. For this present work I have raided whole sections of my former books no longer in print, other work has been brought up to date, and fugitive contributions to *The Times, The Sphere, Lloyd's List, The Trident*, journals of the Port of London and other institutions have been unearthed and refurbished. This material, old and new, is now presented in some sequence.

London River, the old seamen's name for the Thames below bridges, between the Pool and the sea, has been my province. Above bridges the River of London seems to lose much of that rumbustious romance, and in the main I have left that story to better qualified historians. Here, then, are pictures of the middle and lower tideway before containers and other innovations in sea carriage swept away much that had endured for centuries.

L. M. Bates

For Pippa, Rachel, Liz and Sarah

Upper Pool to Brunswick Wharf   1

A LITTLE reflection reveals that the strong allegiance to their river shown by all good Thamesmen is really an appreciation of the tide that made this otherwise comparatively lightweight trickle (compared, that is, with the Amazon and the Mississippi) the world's most famous river. There are tides and tides; the tide of William Sharp that comes "with a shout", and Tennyson's tide that "moving seems asleep, too full for sound and foam . . .". Thames tides are in Tennyson's category, and there is no doubt that without the gentle twice-daily nudge from the sea, the waters of the London River would never have borne the world's fleets and the capital would have been elsewhere.

Poets, painters and lyricists have always favoured the ebb tide as the one most pregnant with drama, and, indeed, even in these days of travel faster than sound, the ebb tide is still the principal vehicle for the outwardbound spirit and the attendant atmosphere of release, adventure, separation and poignant farewells. The artist senses what the seaman knows—that the ebb tide epitomizes both the rewards and the exactions of the sea.

Join me in a typical ride down an ebb tide in, say, the late thirties. We will start in the Upper Pool near Tower Bridge and voyage down to Tilbury in Essex. It is nearing dark on an uncouth November day. There is every promise of unpleasant weather "outside", and we are thankful that our passage down river is to finish well inside the estuary. No such comfort sustains the two colliers, flying light (unladen) and bound for the North East Coast. These two ships that tail on astern of us are "flatirons", vessels specially designed to pass under bridges to reach up-river gas works and power stations. Their masters navigate with a nice calculation of the depth below their keels and the clearance between their superstructures and bridge soffits.

This Upper Pool bears a great burden of London's history. Dominating the scene is the Tower of London, but the sad ghosts who have passed through Traitors' Gate are too well known to need recording here. Not so well known is that Billingsgate is an old Roman port, the work of Belinus, the Roman civil engineer reputed to have built Stane Street.

Tradition for long had it that the two Dutch schuyts that formerly swung at moorings off the fish market and did a thriving

1

trade in imported eels had been granted free moorings in return for services rendered to London during the Great Plague of 1665. But when the moorings were relinquished, no trace of any such grant could be found, and it seemed that generations of wily Hollanders had held on to the buoy by squatters' right.

Downstream of Billingsgate is the Custom House, on a site at which Government revenue had been collected for some six hundred years. In the background is the seventh-century Berkyngechirche, All Hallows by the Tower. We shall find that it encapsulates much of London's story from Roman times to the blitz.

On the south side of the Upper Pool stands the long line of Hay's Wharf warehouses. Flanked by Tooley Street, this was then the centre of London's provision trade. The site has three hundred years of links with old London Bridge and Southwark. China clippers used to berth there, and Shackleton's *Quest* sailed from there on his last tragic passage to the Antarctic. As we steam past, we shall almost certainly see a Russian ship alongside. Named after prominent revolutionaries these vessels sometimes arrived under another name following the latest political purge.

Tubby Clayton has not yet created the Children's Beach below the Tower ramparts, but when it came into being, Stepney mums and their children reached it via the former accommodation ladders of the ill-fated *Rawalpindi*. Now we come to Tower Bridge, the most significant symbol of London's port. (See Chapter Five.) Below the bridge, the ravages of today's Dockland Development begin in earnest and the modern Wapping Waterfront, with its space-age offices and dwellings, bears little relationship to what we see on our trip in the nineteen-thirties.

In the background of the north bank are the London and St Katharine Docks. West of them and almost in the shadow of the bridge we see Irongate Wharf, now absorbed by the Tower Hotel. This was the home of the "Navvies", ships of the General Steam Navigation Company, which claimed to be the world's oldest ocean-going steam navigation company. It mainly dealt in Continental trades, notably with Spanish, French and Italian wine. But equally famous were its "Butterfly" vessels. These ships, formerly paddlers but later screw-driven, took hundreds of thousands of East Londoners for an annual day's holiday to Southend, Ramsgate, Margate or Clacton. Crab teas and ever-open bars were part of the treat. At the outbreak of war, they crammed their decks with children being evacuated to safer parts. They played an important part in the Dunkirk evacuation and their broad decks made them very suitable as floating gun platforms. Equipped with imported Bofors anti-aircraft guns manned by Army gunners, these vessels were known by the Senior Service as "The Pongo Navy", Pongo being the Navy's affectionate slang for a soldier.

Before the war the PLA used to hire one of these ships for their public River and Dock Cruises, and this was the background of a well-known river character. Old Jock, an elderly Scottish dock policeman, went on these cruises for first-aid duties. On his first trip, he consumed a traditional crab tea in the saloon, but his Scottish soul was shaken when he was presented with a bill. It was the start of a long tideway feud. The steward claimed that Jock was not a member of the crew and so not entitled to a meal. Jock claimed that he was. He used to station himself at the top of the companionway leading to the saloon, and when passengers asked where they could get a cup of tea, he used to say, loud enough for the steward to hear: "Weel, ye can get a cup o' tea o' sorts doon below, but as for myself, what likes tea what *is* tea, I wait till I get ashore."

Between the St Katharine Dock and the river there was formerly a dark canyon between cliffs of po-faced warehouses. Here in the nineteen-thirties was South Devon Wharf. If you are one of the readers who have laughed over the yarns and philosophy of the *Night Watchman*, you will regret the passing of this wharf where lived W. W. Jacobs and which was the background for many of his stories. (See Chapter Eleven.)

Until London's seaborne trade moved downstream to Tilbury, Tower Bridge opened for the passage of ships on average fourteen times a day. This picture shows a small coasting vessel outward bound and, on the left, one of the now vanished Butterfly fleet which formerly took thousands of Londoners down to the sea for a day's outing.

HMS Belfast *at her permanent moorings in the Upper Pool. A feature of the river from relatively recent times, she provides a popular visit for those "doing" London.*

We next pass Carron Wharf, now hidden beneath houses and flats. We see one of the Carron Line ships alongside. Note the cannon ball incorporated in the topmast, signifying this company's connection with the carriage of munitions of war during three centuries. The old-time naval gun, the carronade, was made at and took its name from the Carron Ironworks in Stirlingshire.

Reverting to modern times for a moment, this area has recently acquired a link with the United States. For many years, the London Royal Naval Reserve was housed in its headquarters and drill ship, HMS *President*, moored off the Embankment near the Temple. The first *President*, built in 1794, was an American 44-gun frigate. Later, as a commerce raider commanded by Stephan Decatur, she became a menace to British commercial shipping. She was eventually captured in 1814 by a British squadron after a fiercely fought battle. In those days, captured major warships were taken into the Royal Navy and the names of those that had fought gallantly were absorbed into the Navy list. In 1988 the London Royal Naval Reserve came ashore and hoisted the white ensign at President's Quay on the redeveloped Wapping waterfront.

Back to the nineteen-thirties. With memories of Dibdin's old song in our ears, we watch Wapping Old Stairs slide past. At the top is the old pub, The Town of Ramsgate. Formerly The Red Cow, it sheltered the infamous Judge Jeffreys who had presided at the Bloody Assize after the battle of Sedgemoor. His hiding place was discovered by vengeful London apprentices just as he was preparing to flee the country. He was seized and carried to the Tower, where he died miserably. The original stairs were worn away by countless seamen and watermen, including the feet of Nelson, and for long have been neighboured by a later stairway almost as venerable.

Somewhere along this part of the river was Execution Dock. It was never a dock in the modern sense but a grim seamen's joke about the place where many pirates finally ended their voyaging, and was merely a gibbet on the foreshore. After a hanging, the body was left on the gallows to be submerged by three successive tides as a warning to passing, possibly mutinous, mariners. Captain Kidd was executed here in 1701. Ordered to destroy the pirates infesting trading routes, he was himself accused of piracy and ended his life here at Wapping.

The chain and padlock which secured the condemned men was brought up from the river by a PLA dredger in the early nineteen-thirties; they were judged authentic by the British Museum. It was about that time that I visited The Turk's Head in Wapping High Street, an unpretentious little pub left stranded when an older Wapping vanished under waterside warehouses. Built some three hundred years ago and closed shortly before the last world war, it had traditionally supplied a quart of ale to each pirate on his way to execution.

Next, Wapping Police Station swims into view; since then it has been rehoused on the site of the former Morocco and Eagle Sufferance Wharves. This is the headquarters of the Thames Division of the Metropolitan Police. Quite separate from PLA dock police, the Thames Division patrols the river from Dagenham to Teddington, where the tide ends. Relations between the Force and tideway workers were still guarded in my early days in the river, but they grew more friendly with the passing years. The great wave of river piracy in the previous century had left a faint legacy of "findings, keepings", but in late years the police began to claim that the tidal river was among London's most law-abiding areas.

In the days when coal loomed large in river trades and lighters full of it swung at buoys, a hard-up waterman might be tempted to help himself, especially in the grip of wartime rationing. Questioned by the river police about the pile of coal in his skiff, he would indignantly assert that he had legitimately "drudged" it from the river bed beneath a coaling berth. If it had been stolen from a barge and had merely had a bucket of water thrown over it to make good the story of "drudging", the bottom layers would be

Fast, modern craft of the Thames Division of the Metropolitan Police operate from their station at Wapping in the Upper Pool.
Courtesy: Metropolitan Police

still dry. The police would accordingly turn over the pile. This river force had its own macabre lore about the places where suicides' bodies, the sport of tidal currents, were likely to come ashore.

Still further downstream in this Wapping waterfront we see St John's and King Henry's Wharves, now disappearing under development. Here was the base of Sun Tugs, craft of the old-established firm W. H. J. Alexander Ltd. Their managing director, Charles Alexander, will feature large in the section of this book dealing with the people of the river.

The story of London's tugs is worthy of a book to itself; it tells of enterprise, history, adventure and romance. (See Chapter Fifteen.)

Our attention is now diverted to a wharf on the north bank from which a Dutch schuyt is pulling out. These clog-shaped craft achieved almost a monopoly of the British coasting trade before the war. A family home as well as being a freighter, they were crewed by, say, father at the helm, one or two sons as deck hands, and mother hoisting her washing on a halliard to dry. They were cheap to run with a simple oil engine which said "kertonka kertonka" up and down the tideway. On the south bank we see the old pub, The Mayflower, named for its supposed association with the departure of the Pilgrim Fathers. (See Chapter Six.)

River traffic is beginning to increase as the tide gathers strength, but, for the moment, most movement comes from a small fleet of swans. These birds have an uncanny intelligence service and they have obviously received news of an expected grain ship at one of the south side wharves, for they are crossing over from their usual loitering ground near Shadwell Pierhead. They are anticipating fallout from the grain elevators. Although for many years there had been more swans in the industrial reaches than in the rural Thames upsteam, I felt that they were in their wrong setting; their home should rightly have been lily-fringed, limpid and gracious, not these tug and collier infested waters which they now haunted like former princesses seeking a living in a post-revolutionary world.

On the north bank near the end of the Lower Pool and near the Shadwell entrance to the London Docks is another old riverside pub, The Prospect of Whitby. When I first knew it, it was a typical waterman's hostelry, but in the nineteen-thirties it is already beginning to become a sophisticated night spot. (See Chapter Six.)

We have now turned south into Limehouse Reach. The banks we have passed have been especially rich in old watermen's stairs; some disappeared in the blitz; some have been or are being absorbed in new development; others still remain. Many of their names—Prince's Stairs, Alderman Stairs, Cherry Garden Stairs, Fountain Stairs, Pelican Stairs (perhaps commemorating Francis Drake's famous ship, which was only renamed *Golden Hind* after he had circumnavigated the world), Pickle Herring Stairs—were colourful but inconsequential punctuation marks in what was then mainly a squalid and utilitarian background.

We are reminded that in pre-war days the number of passengers or the tonnage of cargo to be carried were not the only influence in ship design; ahead of us, pulling off a wharf, is a dazzling lovely under the Swedish flag. A *Sun* tug dances attendance, leading her, as it were, by the hand. Her lines are sweet, simple and modern, and I feel with all the illogical insularity of a chauvinistic islander that this symphony in green and cream ought to be under the Red Ensign.

On the south bank we catch a glimpse of Nelson's Dry Dock, once the home of Bilbe and Company, owners of the Orient Line of clippers to Australia, forerunners of the Orient Line of steamers, later merged with the P&O. (See Chapter Sixteen). In 1854, one of the Bilbe partners bought a Dutch galliot, the *Reinauw*

Engelkins, of only ninety gross tonnage. In her he sent his brother-in-law, an impoverished clergyman, and his very large family to Melbourne. The little ship is believed to have been the smallest commercial passenger-carrying vessel to make the 12,000-mile passage; she finished her days as a hulk in New Zealand.

On the north bank we now see the King Edward VII Memorial Park with its plaque: "This tablet is in memory of Sir Hugh Willoughby, Stephen Borough, William Borough, Sir Martin Frobisher and other navigators who, in the latter half of the 16th century, set sail from this reach of the River Thames near Ratcliff Cross to explore the northern seas."

Behind Sir Hugh Willoughby looms the greater shadow of Richard Chancellor whose name, for some unknown reason, has been omitted from the plaque. Chancellor sailed as Pilot General in Willoughby's expedition of 1553 which sought a northern short cut to India. The ships of this expedition were dispersed by gales, and Chancellor failed to find them at an agreed rendezvous. Arriving in the White Sea, he went overland to Moscow and there received many valuable trading concessions from the Czar. When he returned to this country, his reports resulted in the formation of the Muscovy Company, the first of the chartered companies of merchant venturers.

Next to the park is Regent's Canal Dock, now awaiting redevelopment. Leading from it is Limehouse Cut, still, in the nineteen-thirties, helping to distribute the Port's oversea trade. Before we began this sample voyage, I went a short way up the Cut to visit the Royal National Lifeboat Institution's central stores depot. From it flowed much of the equipment and technical know-how that sustained this unique service.

The store actually contained a rigging loft, probably the last one in use along London River. I saw there old boatswains, artists with manilla and hemp, busy with marlinspikes on giant springs, fat fenders, hawsers and heaving lines. Stacks of hides awaited conversion into crafts' bow puddings. A coil of tanned towing and tripping line led me to a corner where, with thoughts of the intrepid Captain Voss, in whose memoirs sea anchors figure so largely, I found a number of canvas drogues. In other parts of the store were cleats and fairleads, lamps, oilskins, life jackets and all those delightful items which help to explain the way of a man with the sea. Another floor was devoted to propaganda, and the hill of collecting boxes would have lit up the eyes of the most bewitching collector who ever made us lose our loose change and the morning train.

From this depot, RNLI experts used to travel to lifeboat stations all around the coasts. Sometimes craft were actually equipped and tested at this little shipyard, and it boasted its own miniature dry dock. Powered machinery helped to make gear, stoving and enamelling were done, and there was a busy carpenter's shop.

An amphibious tractor was available to help difficult launchings, but during the summer months before holidays abroad became popular an abundant supply of voluntary manual labour was usually available. I was surprised to find much metal equipment left in that bright condition known to seamen as spit and polish. "It's for the seaside crowds," explained my guide. "They all visit the lifeboat station on show days." The landsman likes winking brasswork; he likes his boats to look like boats. Soon after the war the depot transferred to Boreham Wood, a loss to Thames's lore and lure.

Back to the south bank of the main channel, we pass the Burning Ground, known to rivermen as Condemned Hole. Established early in the eighteenth century by HM Customs for the destruction of seized contraband, it had long since become the headquarters of the Receiver of Wreck for London. Here were stored pieces of cargo salvaged from the river or brought in by ships from the sea, all officially described as either flotsam, jetsam or lagan*. A little further downstream on this south bank is the Greenland Entrance Lock of the Surrey Commercial Docks. In their heyday, these docks had an atmosphere in complete contrast to the other urban groups.

Our scrutiny of the banks is momentarily diverted by what seems an unbroken line of craft: tugs and barges taking up the complete channel ahead of us. We look uneasily at our skipper, for we can see no opening in the line and he makes no effort to ring down our speed and avoid overtaking. But the line of craft so much resembles a forward rush that I am reminded of a Rugby football ancient who, more years ago than I like to count, gave me sage advice; he said: "If you see a little hole, however small, in their line, go for it and you'll get through." Sure enough, a little hole appears between two of the tugs; it grows bigger as we near it and eventually we slip through with many feet to spare.

Our skipper is an impassive figure who seems to take in the course and speed of overtaking vessels astern of us without taking his eyes from craft ahead. Tugs crossing his bows are no more trouble than flies. A trick of the tidal current flirts a dumb barge broadside across our stem and threatens to pin us against a barge road, but the wheel spokes drip unhurriedly through his hands like the beads of a marine rosary, and we pivot on our heel and are

*Flotsam: goods that remain floating after a wreck. Jetsam: goods sunk after being jettisoned to lighten ship. Lagan: goods jettisoned and sunk but buoyed in the hope of recovery.

away without so much as an inch of paint being scraped. And all the time he continues slowly and evenly to tell us some piece of droll river scandal which, following the usual pattern, had begun at Aden in piece, ranged as far afield as Esquimalt in time of war and would, I knew instinctively, end at Gravesend or Rotherhithe.

On the north bank we now find a rich haul of interest in Narrow Street, Limehouse. Today, it is becoming a fashionable residential area, but in the nineteen-thirties it was an unpretentious little street that has nevertheless run through much of our island sea story. Raleigh walked it to look at his ships. Humphrey Gilbert and William Borough lived in or near it; William Pett built his *Greyhound* there and lived nearby; Duncan Dunbar and James Cook, names which carry more weight in the antipodes than in modern Limehouse, lived there. And, according to J. G. Birch (*Limehouse through Five Centuries*, published 1930) the family of Jerome K. Jerome (*Three Men in a Boat*) lived in Narrow Street. Perhaps typical of this country's prodigality in giving away its technological skills, Admiral Togo worked at a Narrow Street shipyard in 1870 and took what he had learned back to the infant yards of Japan.

The riverside here matches the history. The old unspoiled waterman's pub in Narrow Street, the Grapes, claims to have links with Dickens, but 98 Narrow Street has similar and perhaps stronger claims. In the nineteen-thirties, No 98 was part of the barge-repairing works of W. N. Sparks and Sons—a long river frontage of rambling buildings and waterworn stone, the longest stretch of commercial Thames-side almost unchanged from the London of more than two centuries ago. I had many times voyaged past its cavernous barge yard, which provided a dramatic, almost occult, scene where distant troll-like figures worked in shades dimly lit by the blue spray of welding sparks.

The most easterly house held by the firm was Number 100. When I visited it, I found in its cellar a mysterious bricked-up archway. This should, of course, have inspired stories about smugglers, but in truth no one had the slightest idea as to its original function. Number 98 was formerly The Two Brewers, a pub which features in Chapter Six.

Upstream of No 98 is Duke Shore—a flight of watermen's stairs licked smooth by countless tides, and an open patch of foreshore. Beside the head of the stairs I explored an old wooden watch house which almost certainly dated from the seventeeth century. Mr Birch records that in 1682, Robert Hemlington, the constable, was instructed to install a new whipping post there. In 1872 the rents from No 96 were bequeathed to St Anne's Church, Limehouse, for the maintenance of the parish clock and bells.

In No 94 was the main office of Sparks'. Here I was shown

some bricked-up ovens and I hoped that I might have rediscovered the lost birthplace of the famous blue-and-white Limehouse chinaware. But it seems they were merely relics of a former sugar bakery, probably founded by Hanoverian bakers, immigrants early in the last century.

No 92 was once The Watermen's Arms, but neither history nor local legend has anything to say about it. No 90, at the western end of Sparks' works, appeared to be the oldest of this group. It was here that a workman found a spade guinea and a doubloon. Five generations of the Sparks family, covering more than one hundred and fifty years, had worked in the river. The two directors, both with a lifetime of barge work behind them, had memories of vessels they called billyboys, of square-rigged ships, schooners and other types of vessels. And they talked of the bowsprits poking through the windows of Limehouse taverns.

After the war, when the last of the Sparks had left Limehouse, the premises were taken over by the lighterage firm of W. J. Woodward Fisher. The late Mrs Woodward Fisher was a well-known riverside character who ran her business in a very efficient, if somewhat autocratic, manner. A woman manager appears to have been unique in the long story of the London lighterage trade. Dockland development has taken over the interior of the old buildings but, heaven be praised, the frontage is guarded by a preservation order.

Below Duke's Shore is a little tidal inlet, Limekiln Creek. On its western bank in the nineteen-thirties we could see Limekiln Wharf (now taken over by modern dwellings and a shop). Here were the kilns that gave Limehouse its name. The industry had been carried on from medieval times until recently. Before the First World War, Limehouse was the kind of place where policemen patrolled in pairs, for it was the sort of Chinatown portrayed in some of the less-inspired silent films of that period. Certainly, there were opium dens and gambling joints where Asian seamen from the nearby docks found entertainment. A lurid case of drugs and murder involving a young British actress created so much publicity that authority took action to rehabilitate the area. At the time, local gossip said that all the wrongdoers had migrated to Soho, a claim hotly denied by the charming little restaurants there. Before the war, the firm of W. B. Bawn in the West India Dock Road had the figurehead of an old-time Jack Tar on the roof of their premises. All over the seven seas, Asiatic seamen used to describe Limehouse Causeway as "the street opposite the sailorman".

We must pause in our nineteen-thirties trip to look at Dunbar Wharf on the western bank of the Creek. Here is a treasure house of maritime memories tended by the wharf owner, F. V. Smythe. When I visited the wharf, I found reflections of the port's

The roof figurehead, formerly a signpost to Chinese seamen in the West India Dock Road.

vicissitudes during the last half century. Sixty years as a Thames-side character had endowed him with a rich store of Limehouse traditions from the days when it was the home of tall ships trading to Australia and the Far East. He had seen the gradual decline of old-style merchant adventurers before the advance of the limited liability company, the passing of the halcyon days of colonial expansion and the dawn of our present age of grim competition and unrelenting speed.

Smythe was a good business man who kept his wharf up to date with electric power and modern labour aids, but he also had a jealous regard for the many relics of "sail" remaining on the premises. It was here that Duncan Dunbar founded his famous fleet a century and a half ago. The better-remembered Duncan Dunbar Junior was born at the wharf in 1804. Equipment for the old square-riggers was nearly all made in situ and I was shown thick layers of Stockholm tar and rope yarn adhering to the floor of the loft where rigging had been served and tarred. It was only comparatively recently that wine vaults under the wharf had been demolished.

These vaults had been important features in the Dunbar fortunes, for the early Australian pioneers, unaccustomed to fierce southern sunshine, developed a generous thirst which needed an ocean of British bottled beer. Most of this beer was brewed at the Barley Mow Brewery at Limehouse and stored in the Dunbar vaults until it could be shipped. The bottles had a special label embodying the Dunbar house flag, and envious rivals said that the Dunbar fortunes floated to success on Taylor Walker's ale.

When the second Dunbar died in 1862, the business and many of the ships were taken over by Edward Gellatly, the wharf manager, who founded the well-known firm of Gellatly, Hankey and Sewell, still flourishing as Gellatly, Hankey. Young Smythe entered the service of this firm in 1871, coincident with a period of expansion and increased prosperity. The firm sent sailing ships and steamers to all parts of the world, the vessels loading at Limehouse Buoys or the East India Docks, some of the cargo being shipped from Dunbar Wharf. It was in those days that Smythe met and worked with comparatively unknown men who later became household names in the shipping world: Sir Charles Cayzer, founder of the Clan Line, the first Mackay (Lord Inchcape) of P&O, and others. He remembered the protests by India Merchants in London when it was proposed to send mails through the new Suez Canal instead of by the existing overland route which then linked the Mediterranean and the Red Sea.

He cherished reminders of those and earlier days at the Wharf. On the walls of the main office were portraits of the two Dunbars and a painting of the Dunbar house flag. He had a fine collection of pictures of ships of the Dunbar fleet. A painting of the full-rigged ship *Duncan Dunbar*, which for several years carried troops to India and Australia, was a reminder of the once well-known writer Clark Russell who served in her.

Three of his pictures connoted sea tragedies. A fine clear drawing of the *Dunbar*, one of the fliers of the fleet and favourite vessel of the old shipowner, commemorated her loss in 1857 off Sydney Heads. Only one seaman was saved out of a complement of 122 passengers and crew. Another picture portrayed the *Cospatrick*, destroyed by fire in 1874 outward bound for Australia. Only five men survived after much suffering in a ship's boat. A tragedy nearer home was recalled by a picture of the *Northfleet*, built at Gravesend. With a full complement of emigrants for Australia, she anchored off Dungeness, and there, during the night, was rammed by a steamer which backed off and fled. A Gravesend tugboat, *City of London*, was lying nearby and the deck boy, keeping anchor watch, saw rockets. He called his skipper, remarking that the ship seemed in a great hurry to get a pilot. But the tugmaster knew better; he ordered steam and paddled down to the wreck. He saved many lives, but more than a hundred were drowned.

Not all Smythe's pictures had tragic associations. A picture of the *Alumbagh* inspired a story about a soldier who, having fallen overboard, was given up for lost by the boat searching for him, but who was then found foul of one of the oars. A picture of the *Edwin Fox*, the last of the fleet (she ended her days as a New Zealand hulk) reminded Smythe of a deputation by a new crew complaining of a ghost in the fore 'tween deck space—the ghost was a huge white figure wearing a top hat: Edwin Fox himself. It turned out to be the ship's damaged figurehead awaiting repair. A list of ships of the Dunbar fleet showed that most were named after battles and that despite the firm's own yards at Howrah and Moulmein the majority had been built by Laing of Sunderland. Smythe died before the end of the war, but if residents of the new developments there hear the rattle of blocks and the creak of cordage, or see moonlit shadows of tall masts and square-rigged yards, they will know that he keeps watch on an historic site which he revered.

Leaving the creek astern and still on the north bank, we next see Union Dry Dock. When the first dock here was built in about 1845, the owners solved the problem of providing firm foundations by using the old East Indiaman *Canton*, which they sank in position and pinned into the ground. Decks, beams and carlings were removed and her stern was replaced by lock gates, the ship herself becoming the dry dock. This was almost certainly the *Canton* which in 1797, in company with an unescorted fleet of other merchantmen off the coast of Java, hoisted the colours of a British warship and bluffed a force of hostile French frigates into retreat.

13

There is (or was) a picture of the incident in Lloyd's. She served as a dry dock until 1898, when she was replaced by a more conventional structure. Among the vessels overhauled there was the *Cutty Sark*. After the last war, the dock was in turn superseded by a modern slipway for tug and barge works. And now Dockland Development has its eye on the old site.

Back to the south bank; we have missed the old pub, the Dog and Duck, between the Greenland Entrance and the old South Dock entrance. (See Chapter Six.) But downstream of the Surrey Commercial group we are in time to see Deptford Creek, waterway of splendid memories, though little of the fabric of former glories remains. Here began the Corporation of Trinity House, the building of Henry VIII's Royal Dockyard (some of which was fortuitously revealed by bomb damage), its association with Drake and other Elizabethan adventurers; here took place Pepys's struggle against dockyard peculation; here famous shipbuilders built famous wooden ships; explorers sailed from here to found new colonies.

Deptford was the ground from which, perhaps more than any other, grew the British Empire. And if that word is now unpopular, let us remember that Deptford helped to export Parliamentary democracy and the ideals of the British Commonwealth. By luck, or perhaps with a superb appreciation of historical links, the London base for the United States Navy during the build-up for the invasion of Europe in 1944 was established at Deptford, little more than a stone thrown from where Drake had been knighted. When flying bombs and rockets devastated part of the area, US sailors and marines joined local forces in digging citizens out of their blitzed homes. Where are they now, those friendly foreigners who set Cockney lungs puffing Lucky Strike cigarettes, Cockney jaws revolving round gum, and distorted Cockney accents with transatlantic idioms? Their kind hearts are still remembered with affection by those few older inhabitants remaining in the district.

Back to the north bank, we now approach a stretch of the riverside, formerly known as Coconut Stairs and Britannia Wharf. Between them, in 1859, Isambard Brunel launched the *Great Eastern* after she had stuck on the slipway for some three months. Brunel thought big—too big, for she was designed far in advance of her time and was, almost inevitably, a commercial failure. But she did lay the first part of the Atlantic cable, a link which did much to encourage the two nations to think alike. The cable itself was made on Thames-side—the deep-sea sections by the Telegraph Construction and Maintenance Company at East Greenwich, and the shore ends by Henly's W. T. Telegraph Works Company at North Woolwich. The remains of Brunel's slipway, where the ship was launched, could be seen at very low water.

Where Limehouse Reach merges into Greenwich Reach, memories of the vanished glories of Deptford give place to the Greenwich story, hardly less famous. The jewel of the waterfront and, indeed, of all London River, is the Royal Naval College. Many times I have voyaged round the curve from Limehouse Reach and watched the four blocks of the College sweep into view, two by two, their aloof and spacious dignity mellowed by the graceful arc of the river. In the background is the National Maritime Museum with its pictures and relics of the men and ships that make up the Greenwich story. (See Chapter Seven.)

We are too soon in the nineteen-thirties to see the changes brought about by the blitz. The Greenwich Ship Tavern which we pass is to be destroyed and give place to the land-bound *Cutty Sark*, home and dry for good mainly by the efforts of that devoted lover of sail, Frank G. G. Carr, post-war director of the National Maritime Museum. (See Chapter Ten.) The most celebrated survivor of merchantmen under sail, she was built in 1869 as a square-rigged ship for the China tea trade. The *Cutty Sark*'s figurehead represented Nannie, the witch in Burns's poem *Tam o' Shanter*, a cutty sark, ie, a short chemise, being all that the uninhibited Nannie wore.

The new ship was dogged by bad luck. First on the China run and then in the Australian wool trade, she made slow passages and earned poor freights. A murder, a suicide, mutiny and cholera, as well as a succession of unsatisfactory masters, gave her a bad reputation. Her luck turned, however, when first Captain F. Moore and then Captain Richard Woodger took command. During the next ten years, she beat all the other clippers, including the famous *Thermopylae*.

In 1895 the ship was sold to Portuguese owners. Later, after serving at Falmouth and then in the Thames as a cadet training ship, she was permanently housed at Greenwich after the war. In 1957 she was opened to the public by HM The Queen. The romance of the sea and sailing ships is not dead in this country, and several millions of people have visited her. Among the many treasures on board is a number of old merchant-ship figureheads. We shall note the origins of this collection when we pass Gravesend. *Cutty Sark* has since been joined at Greenwich by *Gipsy Moth IV*, the yacht in which the late Sir Francis Chichester circumnavigated the world single-handed under sail.

Still off the Greenwich waterfront, we pass the Yacht Tavern and its close neighbour, The Trafalgar. Further along this south bank, characteristic of the way Thames combines mellow past with pragmatic present, we see the charming fairy-tale frontage of seventeenth-century Trinity Almshouses nestling confidingly beneath the wall of the utilitarian Greenwich generating station. In

the background, part of the National Maritime Museum, the old Greenwich Observatory, projects the invisible Meridian of Greenwich (0 degrees latitude) up Blackwall Reach of the Thames. We now leave behind us the elegant formality of the Royal Navy for the more homespun story of the Merchant Navy. This was the home of the stately East Indiaman and Blackwall Frigates, both superbly constructed, equipped and manned. Not for nothing did the old seamen say: "All shipshape and Blackwall fashion". After them came the beautiful clipper ships which also berthed in this reach.

Pepys came to Blackwall Reach to take his pick of prize cargo. The Honourable East India Company knew it as a haven where fortunes, sometimes from a single voyage, were realized. Later merchants knew it as a base for their trade exchanges and commodity markets. The East and West India Docks carried on the story. For some three centuries Blackwall Reach was the main buttress of London's overseas commerce. Near the end of the reach, we pass the main entrance to the West India Docks. On the south bank is Blackwall Point, another place where the bodies of executed pirates were left on the gibbet.

A little way downstream of the West India Dock was, in the nineteen-thirties, the Blackwall Yard (now, alas, being redeveloped), which claimed to be the oldest continually working shipyard in the world. Founded in the seventeenth century, it reached its peak during the last century, when the firm of Green and Wigram built superb frigates at and sailed them from the yard. What might have continued as a successful joint undertaking was smashed by a stupid quarrel in which the partners behaved like spoilt children. Everything, ships, gear and stores, was divided; a brick wall was built to bisect the premises, and even priceless old ship models were ruthlessly sawn in half as sacrifices to the god of false pride.

Before their quarrel, Green and Wigram had begun a new line to India and Australia in 1824 with their *Sir Edward Paget*. Their then new house flag consisted of a white square bearing a red St George's Cross. When the ship put in at Spithead, the flag was deemed to be an admiral's flag and the Navy ordered the offending bunting to be struck. Here legend divides. One story has it that a midshipman in the *Sir Edward Paget* climbed aloft, cut off the tail of his blue uniform coat and pinned it over the centre of the flag. Another story says that a blue scarf was used to alter the design. At

Opposite page: *Trinity Almshouses at Greenwich.*

17

any rate, the flag was retained in this new form until the quarrel in 1843. Then Wigram kept the flag as it was, while Green put the cross over the square. In Wigram's form, the old flag came down the years to become the house flag of the Federal Line. Green's version has disappeared from the sea, but we see it on the caissons of the old yard as we pass in the nineteen-thirties. It is also the cap badge of the school named after his foundation.

After the war the late E. W. Green told me that he disbelieved both stories about the flag; that the partners were too much experienced in maritime matters to have chosen an admiral's flag.

In the late nineteen-thirties Arthur Hellyer, then aged eighty-nine, spoke about the Hellyer family, famous carvers of ships' figureheads (including the original *Cutty Sark* head, lost at sea). They had their own workshop at Blackwall Yard and he was apprenticed there in 1866. He used to help rough out designs in the street outside the yard. In those days the yard had beautiful gates said to have been carved by Grinling Gibbons in the reign of Charles II but now long since disappeared. The late H. M.Tomlinson, kindest of friends, Master Thamesman and most neglected author of this century, wrote lyrically about Blackwall and the old yard. (See Chapter Seven.)

Next on the north bank, we see the entrance to the old East India Docks. At the Brunswick Wharfs which then separated the Export Dock from the riverside, we see the derelict Brunswick Hotel built at the beginning of the nineteenth century for passengers and officers of the Honourable East India Company's ships. It was later turned into a hostel for emigrants during the gold rush to Australia in the eighteen-sixties. In the stonework above one of the bow windows the Astronomer Royal of the day had caused the line of the Greenwich Meridian to be cut. We see it in retrospect, for the building was demolished in 1930.

A record of even earlier emigration is the plaque on the dockmaster's house recording what was virtually the beginning of the United States. It states that here, in December 1606, John Smith and a party of 105 adventurers embarked to found the first permanent English colony in America at Jamestown, Virginia, fourteen years before the better publicized Pilgrim Fathers. These pioneers suffered starvation, repeated attacks by Indians, disease, fire and other hazards, but they survived to develop into the mighty world power of today. Smith himself, only twenty-six when he sailed, had already fought as a soldier of fortune in the Low Countries, had been flung from a pilgrim ship as a Jonah, had fought Turkish campions in single combat and had endured some years of slavery.

The three ships in which they sailed would today be considered absurdly small for such a voyage: the *Susan Constant*, one hundred tons, *Godspeed*, forty tons, and the *Discovery*, twenty tons. All three would be lost among the deck cargo of a modern freighter. Despite what must have been almost unendurable conditions in the little ships, they were delayed, probably wind-bound, for some six weeks before they finally got clear of the Downs and set out for blue water. They eventually landed at Cape Henry, Virginia, in April, 1607.

The United States have always paid the Thames proper respect. The plaque was presented to London River in 1928 by the Association for the Preservation of Virginia Antiquities. It was mounted on the wall of the dockmaster's house near where the story had begun. In 1951 the Port of London Authority set up a beautiful little memorial, incorporating the plaque, on the East India Dock pierhead. But vandals stole the symbolic figure of a mermaid which crowned the memorial. Later, the Central Electricity Generating Board, which took over the site for a new power station, erected a modified form of the memorial on the wharf*. We shall find a repercussion of that adventure in Chapter Four.

*At the time of writing, the power station is being demolished and the wharf cleared for redevelopment, but the memorial has been preserved for eventual re-erection.

Lord Waverley, the chairman of the PLA, opening the memorial at Blackwall to the Virginia Settlers. The sculpted mermaid surmounting the memorial was later stolen and dockland development caused the memorial to be removed. The presentation plaque is being held pending reinstatement.
Courtesy: Port of London Authority

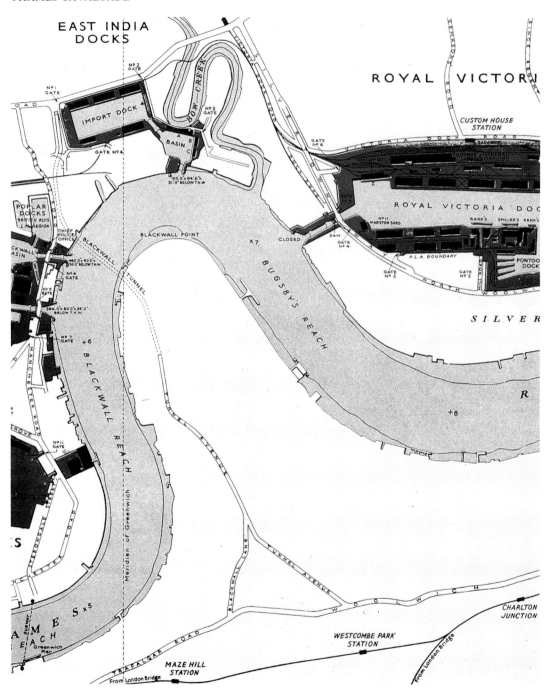

Blackwall Reach to Tilbury   2

FROM Blackwall Reach we turn into Bugsby's Reach. The river has long speculated about the name; who was Bugsby and when did he live? One suggestion is that seamen once knew it as Bugges' Reach, ie, the home of bugges or ghosts emanating from the corpses swinging on the gibbet at Blackwall Point. Then, when prudish early Victorian ladies began taking pleasure cruises down river to Rosherville Gardens at Gravesend, the name, likely to be misheard as bugger, was quietly changed.

Our only place of interest is Blackwall Wharf, fronting the river and, at the side, the entrance to Bow Creek. Here was the depot of the Trinity House Corporation. Equipped with modern engineering workshops, the wharf was usually littered with navigation buoys under repair, and, alongside, a lightship being overhauled was often seen. In 1989 the wharf, no longer needed by the Corporation, was sold to the London Docklands Development Corporation. Trinity House, dating from Tudor times, is responsible for buoying and lighting the English coasts; we shall note its former control of sea pilotage when we reach Gravesend.

Earlier in the nineteen-thirties I was a passenger in the Trinity House steamer *Alert* (lost at Arromanches during the invasion of Europe). We had not long passed Canvey in the estuary when the captain said: "The Nore." I peered through my binoculars and focused on a speck of light downstream. This tiny spot wavering in the lenses was the last main road light on London's marine doorstep.

As we came alongside the old lightship, the *Alert* sprouted fat fenders which added to the chasm over which I had to swing. I was surprised to find how small the lightship was. She was made of wood and was not much larger than a coasting barge. Built in 1839, she remained on station until the war, when, following enemy attacks on such vessels, she was replaced by a Maunsell fort. But that was severely damaged by a fogbound ship, and the Nore Sand is now guarded by a buoy.

Bugsby's Reach now leads us into Woolwich Reach. Both banks are occupied by a variety of industries—smelly soap works, a giant sugar refinery and other undertakings. Let us imagine for a few moments that night has fallen, for, before most of the port's shipping moved downstream to Tilbury, this area was one of

Trinity House, Blackwall Wharf, before it was taken over by the London Docklands Development Corporation.
Photo: Eric Greenhalf

Thames's most dramatic night backcloths. Dimming the tidal red, green and white navigation lights, some of the wharves are blazing caverns across which we may see glide the sombre silhouette of a lighterman tugging at the huge oars of his invisible craft. Harsh and ugly factory chimneys become Whistler's "campanili" and warehouses "palaces in the night". In the background on either side rise cliffs of lighted windows. Ships lying at wharf or buoys are outlined in skeleton form by illuminated ports, masthead lights or derrick arcs. A blood-red advertisement hangs in seemingly miraculous fashion high in the background. Over the inviting glow of this factory window flits a giant menacing shadow of revolving machinery like April clouds. That retort opens a furnace door and a ruddy finger points accusingly at us across the dark water, and the tiny figures of the night shift appear silhouetted against the red glow like swallows in a westering sun.

Woolwich Ferry causes a blaze of light on both banks, while across the river red and white lights move in stately fashion, the marine equivalent of traffic lights, indicating "Cross here." This free ferry service is provided because the county of Kent extends across the river to North Woolwich. In the nineteen-thirties it was owned and run by the LCC, later the GLC, and is now operated by the Borough of Greenwich. With tall, spindly funnels, rather like

poetry of the Thames: the Warp, the Swin, Oaze Deep, Black Deep, the Wallet. These are matched by the names of sands and shoals: Gunfleet, Shingles, Shivering Sand, Maplin. Some of the names reflect their Old English or Norse origins. Gore as in Havengore is from an Old English word meaning a triangular spit of land. Girdler is a corruption of griddle, which the sand so named resembles in shape. Shivering Sand relates to a splinter, as when a glass is shivered. Maplin once had an old causeway across the sands from Wakering Stairs to Foulness Island; this was marked with upended besoms, which gave it the name of Broomway. But brooms made from twigs were known as mapples, which may have led to the name Maplin.

As we steam out, we shall pass the Trinity House navigational buoys, one by one, like cadences in a nautical poem. Some whistle, some ring a warning fog bell. And the names of the swinging, dipping lightships—Mouse, Tongue, Edinburgh, Girdler, Mid Barrow, Nore—are part of the seafaring litany.

I have known the estuary in many moods and have savoured its illimitable skies, misty horizons, its former great variety of ships. There have been boisterous cloud-strewn days when the wind whipped the water, and other days when the grip of winter merged sea and sky into a cold grey wilderness, moonlit nights when evanescent shadows suggested science-fiction vessels, nights so black that the shifting lights on sea and land inspired new respect for the mariners' navigation. Best of all were summer dawns when ships took on fresh life with the sunrise.

The tidal traffic; in the upper reaches of those days so concentrated that ships seemed to jostle each other, out here was dispersed into distant pillars of smoke, or nearer at hand so dwarfed that Cunarders could look like coasters. Most of the big ships outward bound—P&O, Orient, Cunard, Ellerman's, Union-Castle and others—were heading down Channel for the open sea. Smaller vessels—colliers, for the north-east coal ports, ships making for Denmark, Norway and the Baltic—were set on a north easterly course. And always there were local craft—bawleys trawling for shrimps, pleasure bob-a-nob launches, summer yachts out of Westcliff and Southend, butterfly paddlers on day trips, and sometimes, a lone warship making for the Medway and Chatham Dockyard.

For romantic me, these estuary waters became an affair of the heart, a frontier, the high road to China. Air travel has killed the romance of travel, stifled curiosity about far off places and the ends of the earth. And, as my friend Tomlinson maintained, curiosity has done more for human progress than the struggle for bread. For ship lovers, the horizon beyond the Nore still beckons.

★

Opposite page, above:
The Great Nore Tower, a war-time anti-aircraft fort, approximately on the site of the old Nore Lightship.
below: *The former Trinity House Lightship,* Nore, *which is the latest addition to the Maritime Museum at the World Trade Centre, St Katharine-by-the-Tower, London.*

Overleaf: *Plan of Tilbury Docks before the huge container dock was constructed.*
Port of London Authority.

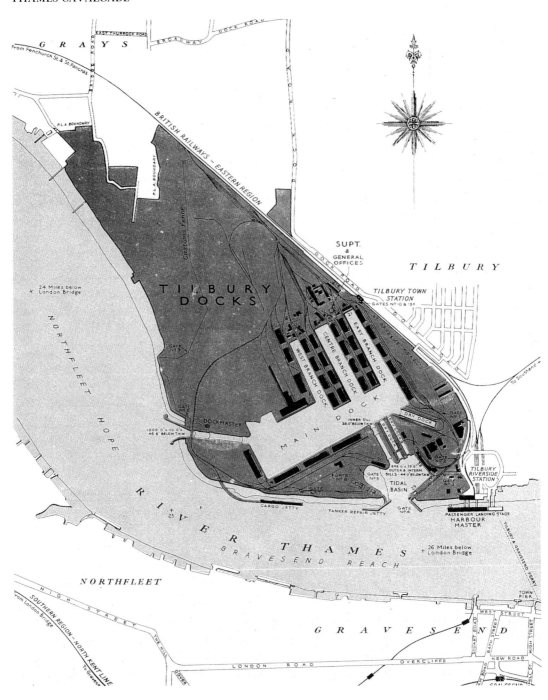

Some Riverside Churches   **4**

FOR some two thousand years the Thames tideway has served as the main conveyor belt of London's history, and much of its priceless and colourful burden has been deposited on the banks of the ancient Pool. Man's irreverence for and indifference to history have permitted many of these riches of the past to corrode and disappear, but here and there in faded parchment, wrought metal and fashioned stone are recorded fragments of the story. The oldest and one of London's greatest surviving original treasure-houses in this respect is Berkyngechirche, All Hallows by the Tower, on the north bank of the Pool. Battle, fire, explosion and the abrasive fingers of time and weather have taken their toll of the structure, and most of it has been renewed more than once through the centuries; but it is sobering to reflect in this transitory age that St Dunstan, and the first Norman King William, Chaucer and Shakespeare must have gazed on parts of its fabric existing to-day.

This grey old church was founded in the seventh century, four hundred years before the Tower of London was built, before England was called England, and when London was little more than a ruined Roman settlement. It would be impossible within the space of these notes to deal in detail with its long story, neither is there scope for a full description of all its relics. It is hoped, however, that the following almost random dips into its past will inspire more Londoners and visitors to see these and many other glories for themselves.

Most of the mellow old structure above ground was destroyed by high explosives and fire during two enemy aerial attacks in December, 1940. This great evil, however, brought some good in its train, for the destruction of 300-year-old panelling behind the organ revealed an hitherto unsuspected Saxon arch, dating from the seventh century, formed of Roman tiles without a keystone. This is by far the oldest arch in London. At the time of the discovery, large fragments of a Saxon stone cross fell from a wall where they had been embedded by the frugal Norman masons who rebuilt the church some eight hundred years ago. There is no doubt that these fragments, now on view in the undercroft, were once part of a noble Celtic monument that stood on Tower Hill before the Normans came. A contemporary but smaller cross was discovered more recently during work on the floor of the nave. But Norman columns, oaken pews polished to a rich glow by the sober Sunday clothes of countless generations of devout Londoners, the ancient clock face singed by the Great Fire of 1666, the organ built in 1675, the venerable Jacobean pulpit, the reredos carved by Grinling Gibbons, the tower stairs up which Pepys hastened to watch with terror the onward sweep of the Great Fire—all these and other centuries-old treasures were swept away in a couple of nights' work by the servants of a régime lasting less than a score of years.

Much, thanks be, remains. Perhaps the chief treasure displayed in the reconstructed church is the superb font cover, a veritable poem in wood from the hand of the master wood carver. Some of the old pulpit survives; its beautiful iron rail is now incorporated in the present pulpit, and its carved wooden door has been converted into a Litany desk. The three famous sword rests, made by those skilful old Sussex ironmasters who have left us their pits and cooling ponds, are intact.

The church brasses are deservedly famous, and many of them are still to be seen. The beautifully engraved figures of John Bacon, "Wolman", his feet resting on a woolsack, and his wife, Joan, shine on the altar steps. John Bacon quitted this life and his export wool trade to the Continent in 1437; and, until the London Dock was closed, past the church where he rests rumbled lorries bearing bales of wool imported from lands undreamed of by John Bacon and his contemporaries. An adjacent plate commemorates Thos. Virby, eighth Vicar, who died in 1453. Poor Virby! The prayer for his soul was mutilated in 1643, as the Churchwardens' Accounts show "Paid Shurlan for cutting the superstitious letters out of the brasses in the Church—16s." In striking contrast to these and a number of other ancient brasses and memorials is a relic of our time, the 1st Fifteen Cap and sword of Sidney Woodroffe, VC, killed in the First World War.

In the north-eastern corner of the church is the restored chantry tomb of Alderman John Croke, citizen and leatherseller, who died in 1477. It still shows remains of the original brasses of Croke, with his seven sons and his wife with five daughters, all kneeling, and his coat of arms above. On it stands the Toc H lamp, first lit by the then Prince of Wales at the Guildhall in 1922. This little symbol represents a movement born of comradeship in tribulation at Poperinghe during the First World War, and it has now spread through all English-speaking countries, resulting in this ancient church virtually becoming the parish church of the western world. This is just as well, for the cost of reconstruction has been far greater than its local parishioners could have borne.

History is, perhaps, more easily grasped in the undercroft,

spared the damage wrought by fire and explosion above ground. Its chapels of St Clare and St Francis date from the fourteenth century; and leading out of the latter is a flight of crumbling, time-worn steps, constructed about AD 675. How many feet have paced reverently down this stairway seeking strength or consolation? How many feet have fled down it seeking sanctuary from the terror above? We shall, more the pity, never know.

In the walk between this chapel and the sanctuary, the resting place of Wm. Laud, Archbishop of Canterbury, 1645, is preserved a section of one of the stout old Norman pillars which upheld part of the roof until they were broken in 1940. In the sanctuary, with its ineffable air of peace in such contrast to the busy City outside, is the altar used by Richard Coeur de Lion in the church of the Knights Templars at Athlit Castle, Palestine. All Hallows has a strong claim to hold the heart of Richard, for it is alleged to have been buried in a "fair Chapel" which this chief of knights errant founded on the north side of the church.

On the north side of the undercroft appears a portion of the wall of the first Saxon church of the seventh century and part of the wall of a Roman house which the church apparently supplanted. In the undercroft, besides the fragments of the old Saxon cross, several examples of Roman pottery and remains of Roman London charred by the vengeful fires of Boadicea in AD 61, all found on the site, are exhibited. To help visitors to visualize the importance of the old church's site, even in the dim ages, a magnificent and highly detailed model of Roman London is on view in the undercroft. It is inspiring to good Thamesmen to note how the church's former neighbouring little water streets then ran down to the Pool on approximately the same sites until destroyed during the blitz.

At the western end of the undercroft are two finely preserved sections of Roman pavement, apparently parts of the Roman house. One section has been relaid, but that under the brick tower of the Commonwealth period is in situ. If Pepys had only known of its existence when he ran up the tower to watch the approach of the fire, his insatiable curiosity might have quenched his fear, and his diary might have been enriched with his speculation on the subject. But, like some of the other discoveries in the undercroft, this pavement lay hidden and unknown until it was uncovered in 1926.

We must reluctantly turn our backs on the other treasures in the undercroft and descend to the treasury, where, behind a steel grille, are the chief jewels of the church*. Here are the church registers, a complete record of the parish's births, marriages and deaths from 1558, the first year of the reign of Queen Elizabeth I.

*Now displayed in the undercroft.

43

In them, good Americans may see recorded the birth of William Penn, founder of Pennsylvania, and the marriage of John Quincy Adams, president of the United States. They may feel sorry for the hand that wrote, and sense the embarrassment behind, the entry for 28 March, 1650: "A cupple being married went away and gave not their names." In the treasury, too, the magnificent gilt communion plate gleams no less brightly than when it was fashioned some three hundred years ago. Coins of the Emperor Nero, miniature plaster heads of Venus, and other relics found on the site are also displayed there. But, to my mind, one of the most striking exhibits in the treasury is a toy stone lamp of the Romano-British period; the little raven-haired Italian who played with it on the ancient hill could have had no more idea of the impermanency of her London than the children whose pathetic toys were seen in the rubble of bonbed London nearly two thousand years later.

In the fire of 1940 the old bells poured down the tower in a molten cascade. In 1948 a new carillon, a gift from Canada, was installed. When, in my time, they rang out some old nursery rhyme through the murk of a London winter's afternoon, the surrounding courts and lanes took on something of the spirit of that older London, the London of overhanging gables and bottle-glass windows, a more colourful, picturesque and infinitely less complex London*.

Having written the foregoing, I am conscious of the inadequacy of the picture I have painted, the many relics passed by without note, the great events unrecorded, the great men ignored. There remained, however, one church treasure which posterity may claim to have been among the greatest—the late Reverend Philip Thomas Byard Clayton, CH, MC, thirty-eighth vicar, founder of the Toc H movement, and indefatigable worker for his church and parish. For many years he had a dream of giving the old Tower and the older church a more worthy setting, and his dream, aided by his parishioners, slowly took shape at the hands of the Tower Hill Improvement Trust, of which the president was Lord Waverley.

The vicar was the friend and chaplain of all Thamesmen, counsellor of princes; an architect of Anglo-Saxon friendship throughout the world; the man who shared the perils of British troops in Flanders during the First World War, and sailed thousands of miles with British tankermen during the Second; the man who, after the war, travelled thousands of land miles seeking help for his broken church.

His closest contact with the actual Thames was the Children's Beach which, with barge loads of sand, he created on the muddy

*Nursery rhymes are no longer played.

foreshore beneath the Tower of London. When he took me to see it, he showed me with pride the former accommodation ladders leading down to the beach. They were inscribed:

Peacetime equipment of the P&O liner *Rawalpindi*. As an armed merchant cruiser under Captain E. Kennedy, RN, she engaged two German battleships in a lone gallant action off Iceland on the afternoon of 23 September 1939 and was sunk, colours flying, with the majority of the crew. In the House of Commons the Prime Minister, Mr Winston Churchill, said: "They must have known as soon as they sighted the enemy that there was no chance for them, but they had no thought of surrender. They fought their guns until they could be fought no more. Their example will be an inspiration to those who come after them."

Noble sentiments, but I wonder if the children who read it and who probably now spend their holidays on the Costas of Spain remember it.

On the beach, the spades and pails, the deck chairs, the splash of oars and sunshine on the sand struck an authentic note. A tousled urchin adventured into the water as far as his rolled up knickers would allow, and he was straining to reach an interesting piece of flotsam when ripples from the wash of a passing tug broke against the seat of his pants. Suddenly a galleon-like figure started to her feet and screamed: "Jim-mee! Jus' you come back at once, you with your bes' trousis on, too." Jim-mee looked guilty and stepped quite two inches before going after the flotsam again.

Three watermen were doing much trade with their skiffs. Ranged along the wall were several perambulators, each one the centre of a party base camp. A be-aproned Stepney Mum guarded each cache of lemonade bottles and picnicalities. All around were ramparts of sand castles and trenches which, despite the admixture of mud in the lower strata, were tended with care.

Downstream, Tower Bridge was having its lunch hour; not until the rising tide had cleared the beach was it likely to be set to work again. In the background, the old Tower seemed to gaze down benevolently. In the foreground, a frieze of heads peered over the promenade rail. Some looked down on the beach, superior in the consciousness of a holiday spent or to come by the real sea; others looked down with pity for the make-believe of the scene.

As Tubby Clayton and I prepared to leave, a tug passing at speed sent in a wash that was greeted enthusiastically by the bobbing little swim suits. But Jim-mee was caught unaware and the wash rose above his thighs nearly up to his armpits. As we climbed the ladder, I heard his anticipatory wail as Mum began to bear down on him.

Alas! The ladders rotted and the water became too polluted and the beach had to be abandoned. There is still poverty in

Stepney, but poverty is comparative and I venture to think that those kids on the beach were richer than those of today. In any case, they have no Tubby Clayton to watch over them.

Before the days of high-rise flats and factory chimneys, the coasting sailors and pilots had an exemplary knowledge of at least the silhouettes of riverside and coastal churches, for those were the buildings most frequently found of a sufficiently distinctive character to provide them with a landmark. History records that most of the venerable piles along Thames-side have played an important part in the ancient business of piloting ships up and down the river. The first of these Thames-side landmarks seen by the homeward-bounders is the fine old Abbey Church of Minster, on the north side of the Isle of Sheppey, a landmark which for more than twelve hundred years has fingerposted the water road to London. But Minster Church has a connection with the Thames more intimate than merely that of functioning as a landmark.

In the church is the tomb of Sir Robert de Shurland, Lord Warden of the Cinque Ports, who died about 1310. The tomb represents a knight in full armour with the figure of a horse's head rising above the waves appearing behind the Baron's right leg. One writer has suggested that the head represents a favourite horse that saved Sir Robert's life by swimming with him across the Swale. Another possible explanation of the head is the grant of all sea wreckage which the Baron obtained from Edward I; this right extended to anything that could be touched by the knight with his lance after riding his horse into the ebb tide. But popular belief has always linked the effigy with the story of Grey Dolphin recorded in the Ingoldsby Legends.

According to this legend Sir Robert was born long before his time, for he would have flourished in certain parts of the world to-day. It begins with a dispute that he had with his friar regarding the disposal of a stray corpse washed up on his manor, a dispute that ended with the breaking of the reverend gentlement's back. Church and Law viewed this as an act of aggression, and a strong force laid siege to the Baron's castle. But Sir Robert refused to be besieged; he made a sortie and drove off the invaders. An appeal was made to the Pope, but the Baron stole a march upon his adversaries by obtaining King's pardon for the deed. How he obtained this pardon centres on the Nore.

Edward I had collected a large number of troops for his war with France and had billeted them around Thames-mouth. Soon after the Baron's escapade, the King was journeying down river in the royal barge to review these soldiers. Sir Robert decided to put off from the shore, meet Edward at the Nore, and obtain the pardon before Church and Law could interfere. According to the

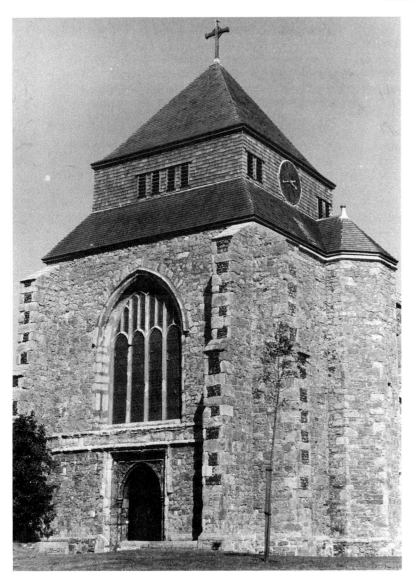

Minster Abbey, Isle of Sheppey. West door and clock tower.
Photo: Norman Silveston

legend, he received a momentary setback when he discovered that the soldiers had broken up all the local boats for their camp fires. But the Baron was a good psychologist and knew the value of stunting; he called for his horse, the famous Grey Dolphin, and dashed into the estuary. For more than two miles, says the legend, the gallant horse fought the tide until it reached the royal barge in the neighbourhood of the Nore. Edward Longshanks was greatly

47

The de Shurland tomb in the Abbey Church of Minster. From The History of the Isle of Sheppey *by Augustus A. Daly. Reproduced by kind permission of the publishers, A. J. Cassel Ltd.*
Photo: Norman Silveston

impressed by the deed, and after extracting a promise of the Baron's service in the forthcoming wars he had the pardon made out there and then. In the meantime Sir Robert cooled his heels by swimming his horse three times round the barge. When the document was safely in his possession he turned the horse towards the shore and eventually landed safely on the beach.

He was greeted by a withered hag, who, true to the conventional withered hag of legend, prophesied his doom, adding that the horse of which he thought so much would be the means to his end. The Baron, hoping to sidetrack fate, drew his sword and killed the horse on the spot without compunction.

It was three years later that Sir Robert de Shurland landed again on his native shore after fighting various campaigns in the service of the King. Marching up from the beach at the head of his men he saw the old hag once more, this time seated on something half-buried in the beach. The Baron rushed forward, but the old lady promptly vanished, leaving Sir Robert looking at her recent perch, which proved to be the whitened skull of a horse. We know by now that gratitude was not a strong feature of the Baron's character and a hearty kick at the skull was all the homage that the memory of Grey Dolphin received. But three years of war without a mediaeval RASC to maintain supplies had severely discouraged the Baron's boots, and one of the teeth from the skull buried itself in the big toe of his right foot. The next day Sir Robert had a high fever and the castle leech found it necessary to amputate the toe. The same evening the Baron died and Grey Dolphin was avenged.

In my copy of the Ingoldsby Legends is a footnote to the story of Grey Dolphin, which reads: "Subsequent to the first appearance of the foregoing narrative, the tomb alluded to has been opened during the course of certain repairs which the church has undergone. Mr Simpkinson, who was present at the exhumation of the body within, and has enriched his collection with three of its grinders, says 'the bones of one of the great toes were wanting, etc.'" Another feature which may or may not have a bearing on the matter is that the vane of Minster Church has a horse's head instead of the conventional feathers, while on the top is the figure of a horse (destroyed during a recent storm and replaced by a cross).

There is no proof of this legendary connection between the famous old church and the best-known place name in Thamesmouth. But for all that, church and river are proven cronies. For more than twelve centuries they have together watched comings and goings in the Port; for more than twelve centuries they have seen the ebbs and flows of London's waterborne history.

I was prompted to visit another church selected for inclusion in this record by the sight of a tug's wash breaking against one of its walls.

There is a peculiar fascination about water-walls, a suggestion of man-made ramparts holding back something elemental and cruel; moated castles, water mills and river and sea embankments all engender a subconscious feeling of security and satisfaction. But not often does one find a church with its foundations lapped by the tide. In the case of most buildings constructed in this fashion, the reason is usually defence or convenience. In the case of St Andrew's Waterside Mission Church at Gravesend it was a question of space, for only by building north and south, instead of the customary east and west, and by making bold use of the low-water foreshore, could the little church be squeezed into its plot.

Thanks to the kindness of the chapel warden, I was enabled during my brief visit to learn much about the history of what is one of the best-known and most picturesque landmarks of the Gravesend waterfront. Its foundations go much deeper than the Thames mud of to-day and began in the latter half of the last century before the church was even contemplated. Gravesend then as now was the outport of the Port of London, and the reach was busy with ships of all types, including many vessels in the emigrant trade. A quick turn round in port was not then so much sought after, and the ships often lay at anchor for several days leisurely waiting for wind, stores or belated parties of emigrants. In addition to this large and changing waterborne population, there was also a floating community of some 80 men, women and children, complete with dogs, cats, chickens and even flowers, who inhabited a number of coal hulks moored in the reach.

About the year 1860 it was pointed out to the Reverend C. E. R. Robinson, vicar of Holy Trinity Church, Gravesend, that the community living in the hulks, who by the nature of their isolated and comfortless existence particularly needed spiritual help, had no parson. The vicar promptly took boat and began regular visits to this strangely situated flock. From these vessels he ventured to the outward-bound ships, especially the emigrant vessels. It was on these often overcrowded and frequently ill-found ships that he eventually concentrated, for the rigours of the forthcoming voyage and the dangers of the undeveloped colonies tempted only those to whom the problems of life in this country had proved overwhelming.

The masters of many of these vessels took a jaundiced view of his visits and he was sometimes met with curses and often with ill-concealed hostility. But he persevered. In these more worldly and materialistic times we can look back with admiration at the doughty old parson who, armed with the courage of his convictions and the gentleness of his faith, braved the jibes and unhelpfulness of hard-bitten ship masters to carry out his duty to poor and often illiterate souls about to sail into the terror of the unknown. Baptisms aboard the emigrant ships were frequent. The settlers were unable to land, and the vicar usually conducted a service in some odd cabin or quiet corner of the ship. No fewer than 535 baptisms of this nature were recorded.

As the waterside mission progressed it became necessary to find headquarters. The problem was temporarily solved by taking over an old Gravesend tavern on the waterfront, the Spread Eagle, and converting it into a mission centre. Among the many activities there was a small school and it is on record that one of the voluntary teachers in the night school was General Gordon. An appeal for a mission church brought an offer from the daughter of

Rear-Admiral Sir Francis Beaufort, KCB, Hydrographer to the Navy; she offered to complete the church as a memorial to her father if the foundations were laid and built up to the level of the road. On St Peter's Day, 1870, at low water (4 am) the foundation stone was laid deep in the bed of the river. The church was consecrated on St Andrew's Day, 1871.

At the time of my visit, its interior was as beautiful as when it was built. The most striking feature was the roof, designed to represent a boat upside down, two cross beams representing the thwarts. Above the altar was a radiant piece of Italian mosaic. The north wall contained a tablet and three windows placed there by Lady Franklin in memory of the crews of *Erebus* and *Terror*, lost in the ill-fated Arctic expedition under Sir John Franklin; the tablet recorded names compiled from the original muster rolls. The church had some splendid glass, most of which escaped damage during the war, despite some uncomfortable close shaves.

The west window depicted the miracle of the 153 fishes, and when built the church was designed to seat that number. It was the custom to ring the church bells when an emigrant ship set out, and many settlers left this country with a last memory of those church bells ringing in their ears.

Sailors and emigrants! It is difficult to think of people to whom faith could be more important. Perhaps if those souls outward bound could have been consulted, the old church might have been saved. But it has been desanctified and at the time of writing still stands, used, I believe, for sporting activities.

Also at Gravesend, St George's Church has a repercussion of those adventurers who sailed from Blackwall to found the English colony in North America. Its archives contain a copy of a petition to King James I in which Thomas Rolfe, John Smith's lieutenant in the historic expedition, requests royal permission to marry the Princess Pocahontas, daughter of the Red Indian chief, Powhattan. The story of how she saved the life of John Smith by shielding him with her own body from her father's squad of executioners is part of American folklore, but although there seems to be some truth in the story it has never been substantiated. What is true, however, is that the princess was converted to Christianity and given a Christian name, that she was taken to England early in the seventeenth century and married Rolfe. But our climate was too much for the poor girl, and the sad sequel is told by an entry in the Parish Registers of the church: "1617 March 21. Rebecca Wrolfe, wyffe of Thomas Wrolfe, Gent., a Virginia lady borne, was buried in ye Chauncell". The story of Pocahontas is told in detail in the St George's Church guide.

In 1952 the church was converted into a Chapel of Unity as a memorial to the little princess. The Union Jack and the Stars and Stripes flew side by side. There are two fine stained-glass windows commemorating Pocahontas presented by the Society of Colonial Dames of America in the State of Virginia, and in the grounds stands a bronze statue of her presented by the people of Virginia in 1958. St George's has now reverted to its former status as Gravesend Parish Church, but the links with Blackwall and the adventures remain.

Statue of Pocahontas in the grounds of St George's Church.

Tower Bridge and   5
Big Ben

MOST cities have a building, status or locality which has become symbolic of the whole in the mind's eye of their exiled sons. But in a city as vast and complex as London it would be difficult to select any one object or place as being representative of the Metropolis; the claims of some suburban town hall or local high street would be contested as hotly as those of the Guildhall or Piccadilly Circus. But for the London riverman there can be no quibbling, for the Tower Bridge against the background of the Pool represents the very spirit of the tideway, and Thames-siders in the world's far places react as emotionally to this picture as to the sound of Big Ben—"London Town", say their ears; "London River", say their eyes.

This is the first or the last bridge across the tidal river, according to whether you are inward or outward bound. Its place in the affections of the Thames-sider has not been usurped by the clean simplicity of more modern bridges upstream. Such is the neglect engendered by familiarity that in more than thirty years of inter-port rambles I had never been backstage of this showpiece of London River until the late nineteen-fifties when I was passed on to the bridgemaster of Tower Bridge, by the courtesy of the City of London Corporation.

I found him as methodical in dealing with writers as he is in maintaining and operating his bridge, and I was first given a tabloid history of the undertaking. Designed by Sir Horace Jones and Sir John Wolfe Barry, it was opened in June, 1894. Day and night since that time, more than half a century before, the machinery had never faltered, a monument to British engineering skill and material. Constructed of steel, it was clothed in a coat of stone in Gothic style to harmonize admirably, whatever the ultra-moderns may say, with the architecture of the adjacent Tower of London. In common with other Thames bridges administered by the City of London Corporation, it was built by and is maintained out of the Bridge House Estate Trust. So this philanthropic bridge not only offers the City ratepayer the finest tourist attraction in London without costing him a penny, but it provides passage for road and water traffic without payment of a toll. Vessels requiring the bridge to be opened give one long and three short blasts (the Morse Code "B") on their sirens and hoist a pennant and black ball, or shape, at the forestay; this signal from vessels proceeding upstream is noted and telephoned to the bridge from Cherry Garden Pier in the Lower Pool, and in the case of vessels bound out is noted direct by the watchman of the look-out staff in one of the control cabins on the upstream side of the bridge.

These points dealt with, I was led into the bowels of the bridge under the roaring road traffic on the south approach. Tower Bridge is worked on the bascule (see-saw to children) principle, each leaf of the bascule, with its counterbalance, weighing 1,100 tons; the two counterbalances are housed underground in two huge caverns. These chambers, one north and one south, are in the form of quadrants, each 50 feet in radius and 44 feet in width, partly below the river bed, and they are in consequence as dank and eerie as any medieval dungeon in the Tower. Peering speculatively into one of those pits, I thought how necessary for visiting authors, particularly fiction writers, to keep a disciplinary grip on their professional imaginations. The Edgar Allan Poe atmosphere is sustained when the bridge is opened, for what appears to be the roof drops slowly down with awful remorselessness.

But the marvel of the bridge is the efficiency and simplicity of its machinery. When the bridge has been cleared of road traffic, already warned by bell signals, four huge bolts locking the centre spans are withdrawn hydraulically. Revolving pinions, also operated by hydraulic power, engage toothed racks at the landward end of each bascule, and within a mere matter of some three minutes 2,200 tons of steel have been moved to provide a passage 200 feet wide for the waterborne traffic to pass. Through this passage go vessels of up to 6,000 tons. Next time you cross the bridge, note the mere cracks where the movable spans join the fixed bridge approaches, and pause to consider whether the doors of your utility house or book-case will meet as closely after more than fifty years of constant operation.

Hydraulic power is generated on the south side of the bridge, where three powerful pumps take turns in pumping continuously into hydraulic accumulators. These were operated by steam when I visited the bridge in the nineteen-sixties, but have since been converted to electricity. The slowly turning twelve-ton flywheel, three revolutions to the minute, and the dignified thrust of shining crankshafts, give an illusion of an old-time ship's engine-room such as M'Andrew knew. The illusion is heightened when the stand-by bells, rather, it must be confessed, more like action station alarms than ship's telegraph gongs, warn the engineer that the bridge is to be opened. And when the great wheel jumps to about eighteen revolutions a minute as the pump restores the lost power, the thud and movement is even more like a ship going full-ahead. The

stored power, remotely controlled by the operators in the control cabins, is piped to the various mechanical key points on both sides of the bridge. The water stored for this giant's work is not wasted, for by an ingenious device it is returned to the circuit again when it has completed its work. The levers in the control cabins are so designed that movement can take place only in the correct order, and they are linked to the signalling systems for road and river traffic.

The high-level bridge, across which hydraulic power mains are carried to the machinery operating the north bascule, and some 110 feet above road level, is no place for height-shy heads. It is reached by hydraulic lifts and provides an almost unsurpassed gull's-eye (or, to conform to the present pattern of feathered visitors, starling's-eye) view of City and river. Inspected from this

Tower Bridge, one of the world's best known bridges, opens its arms to welcome HMS Norfolk on a courtesy visit to London in 1974.

55

eminence, the Tower of London looks incredibly like a boy's toy fort of the superior kind known only to pre-war youth. The bridge crew totals nearly eighty men, and the undertaking is run like a well-found ship, with all a ship's cleanliness and order.

As might be expected, Tower Bridge had a morbid attraction for enemy raiders during the last war, and several attempts were made to destroy it. It was damaged on a number of occasions by direct hits from bombs and near misses by mines and pilotless aircraft, but it was never out of action for more than a short time.

Tower Bridge, with its arms upraised in seeming benediction upon some ship putting out from the Upper Pool, is the insignia of the outward-bound appeal. It is easily the best-known bridge in the world and, at any rate during the tourist season, its opening is a rite of tourism, and the "Gees", "Zos" and "Ba gooms" that accompany the spectacle from Pool-side vantage points are evidence of its continued popularity. Crossing the tideway where the first Londoners crossed, it has been given many poetic titles—"London's Sea Gate", "The Nation's Front Door" and so on. But to me it has always been a symbol of the very spirit of London River. Some of the old machinery I describe is displayed in a small museum open to the public, having been replaced since the nineteen-sixties.

Turning to the other love of the Londoner, Big Ben, it was Jan Struther who, if my memory serves me truly, recorded in one of her poems something of what the great bell meant to a scattered Empire at war. During the fifty-two consecutive nights of the early aerial bombardment of London in the winter of 1940–41 anxious British hearts overseas sent nervous fingers to the tuning controls of their radio in readiness for 9 pm. Night after night the sonorous voice of Big Ben proudly told them that the hard-hit but defiant capital still lived. If a chance bomb had destroyed the clock and had the reassuring chimes failed to reverberate through the world, the enemy would have accounted it a major victory. Big Ben has always been a famous Thames-side feature; in those dark days it became the voice of London.

So it was with reverence that soon after I had visited Tower Bridge I availed myself of an opportunity afforded by the Ministry of Works and E. Dent & Co. Ltd, the clockmakers, to visit Big Ben. Like not a few great ones today, his dwelling has no modern conveniences, and when I had climbed the 295 steps which lead to his eyrie, breathlessness was not entirely due to the mechanical ingenuity of his works.

A striking clock has been a feature of the Palace of Westminster since the thirteenth century. The ancient bell on which the hour was then struck was known as Great Tom of Westminster. It was this bell, and not that of Big Ben as is generally believed, which was reported by a seventeenth-century sentry, charged with having been asleep at his post of duty, as having struck thirteen times; his story proved to be true and he was acquitted. When the old clock tower was pulled down in 1698, the economical Christopher Wren decided to use Great Tom for one of the towers of St Paul's. The bell was, however, broken in transit and had to be recast.

The present clock tower was completed in the late eighteen-fifties, but Big Ben, affectionately named after Sir Benjamin Hall, the rather large First Commissioner of Works, was not installed until 1859. It was begun by Edward John Dent, who died in 1853, and was completed by Frederick Dent. It has since been maintained by his successors, E. Dent & Co. Ltd. The atmosphere of honest craftsmanship attendant on the making of clocks is symbolized by Big Ben, for, although by the time of my visit, its error never exceeded one second of time. Only once had it been out of action through a mechanical defect—a broken pendulum suspension due, it is believed, to the severe shaking it received when the clock tower was hit by a missile during the war, and there was so far practically no wear on the moving parts. The few other occasions that it had been out of order were caused by snow or other unavoidable contretemps, and it had sometimes been temporarily put out of action for overhaul and for changing to and from summer time. The bells were stopped for security reasons during the First World War and on certain state occasions.

The clock maker's representative who kindly accompanied me was indefatigable in explaining the wonders of the mechanism, and I did my best to understand his enthusiastic description. But the inside of even a watch is a mystery to me and I felt that the situation was hopeless from the outset. So these notes must consist of mere superficial impressions rather than a learned paper on the horological aspects of my visit. The clock mechanism weighs five tons and is housed near the top of the tower. Until it strikes the hour or the quarters it shows little evidence of its interest in the passing of time; only the contemplative swinging of the thirteen-foot pendulum and the rhythmic tick show that it is awake. But when it strikes, the mechanism bestirs itself, and its seemingly superfluous wheels, cams and rods follow each other into action like a well-ordered team. The great air brakes fly round like propellers as the bells boom in the belfry above. The operation ends with a screech like an angler's check reel and all is peace again for another fifteen minutes.

Although the winding handles, which formerly employed two men five hours for three days of each week, were still there, the clock was now automatically wound periodically by an electric motor, which took forty minutes to complete the task. It was a considerate little motor, for of its own accord it stopped its activities for a few seconds to allow the quarter bells to strike and then resumed winding. Final regulation of the clock was achieved by adding or subtracting small weights to a tray on the pendulum, and pennies and halfpennies (old money) proved admirable for the purpose. The addition of one penny, for instance, gave four-tenths of a second gain. During my visit I noticed that Big Ben's good behaviour had been purchased for the sum of ninepence-halfpenny (old money).

The dials, twenty-three feet in diameter, are made of cast iron and glazed with flash opal glass; they are washed and cleaned every three years by steeplejacks. In the chambers behind the dials I watched the shadows of the fourteen-foot minute hands and the nine-foot hour hands creeping across minute spaces one foot square and pointing to figures two feet in length. Lighting is effected by ten 100 Watt lamps behind each clock face. The light went out of Big Ben's faces in 1939 when the black-out gripped the Metropolis. Londoners sadly missed the friendly glow, and when the dials were again illuminated in 1945 the crowds in Parliament Square and on Westminster Bridge cheered as for the return of a long-lost friend.

Above the clock room is the belfry. In the centre, snug and paunchy, hangs the great hour bell surrounded by its satellite quarter-hour bells. The principal bell is more than seven feet high, weighs some sixteen tons and is struck by a hammer weighing four hundredweights. This voice of Big Ben has known vicissitudes. The first bell was cast at Stockton-on-Tees in 1856. It was brought to the Thames by coaster and was hung on a gallows in New Palace Yard for protracted testing. Ten months later a crack four feet long was discovered and the bell was condemned. In 1858 it was broken up and recast at the Whitechapel foundry of George Mears. This bell was more successful and it was hung in the belfry in 1859. But within a few months cracks were again discovered. Tempers now became frayed and one of the reactions of this new disaster was a libel action. While dispute and investigation proceeded, the hour was struck on the fourth quarter bell, and the great bell remained silent for the next three years.

In 1862 Sir G. Airy, the Astronomer Royal, was asked for an opinion regarding the advisability of using the bell. He recommended giving the bell a quarter turn to present a different striking surface to the hammer, reduction of the weight of the hammer by half, and the construction of a stout platform immediately beneath the bell to safeguard the tower in the event of the bell disintegrating. Action was taken on the lines suggested, and the bell of Big Ben has served since then without further trouble.

Big Ben, possibly the world's best-known clock. During the blitz its nightly broadcast chimes told the anxious English-speaking world that London still lived.
Courtesy: Museum in Dockland

In the belfry I saw the little cages containing the BBC microphones. The first experimental microphone was housed in cotton wool, which proved excellent nesting material for the birds which haunt the tower. The next microphone was installed in a football bladder until it was superseded by the improved type of microphone now in use. Although the chimes of Big Ben were broadcast all through the 1940–41 bombardment of London, the BBC engineers were often close to failure owing to damage to lines and other incidents. When the flying-bomb attacks began in 1944, a recording of Big Ben's bells was substituted for the live broadcast on security grounds.

The gallery round the belfry gave a magnificent view of the Port of London in the nineteen-fifties. Its river, ships, bridges and buildings showed up clearly without the dwarfing effect obtained from the top of the Eiffel Tower or even the Monument; strangely enough, the belfry looked far more remote from the river than the river looked from the belfry. But the two together are symbolic of man's everlasting pre-occupation with time and tide.

When the Commons' Chamber was destroyed by enemy action in May, 1941, a small bomb or anti-aircraft shell struck the south-west corner of the clock tower and destroyed some of the ornamental iron work and damaged masonry. All the glass in the south clock face was broken, but the clock and its bells were undamaged.

Big Ben has seen many ebb tides sweep out past his feet, and he possibly reflects with some pride that the flow of overseas commerce has been augmented to no small degree by the ties of sentiment of which he has become a symbol. The Director of the New Zealand Broadcasting Service said in 1945 that the sound of Big Ben had attained almost a sacred significance in New Zealand during the war and that when a recording of the chimes was broadcast from all stations at 9 o'clock in the evening the House of Representatives, if in session at the time, took it as a signal to stand in silence as a tribute to New Zealanders serving in the forces.

Kipling might almost have foreseen the drama in those thundering strokes re-echoing in the hearts of British people throughout the world when he wrote in *The Bells* (A School History of England):

> Four o' the clock! Now all the world is still,
> Oh, London Bells to all the world declare
> The Secret of the Empire—read who will!
> The Glory of the People—touch who dare!

For, even if Empire is now a dirty word, Big Ben will have played no little part in preserving those ties which were forged when the old pioneers sailed from the Thames.

Thames-side Pubs 6

IT IS right that a river which for some two thousand years has turned the wheels of national traditions should venerate its waterside taverns, for whereas they served in the past as nurseries for much of the robust spirit of the Thames tides, not a few of them to-day are monuments to the initiative and enterprise so often enlarged within their mellow parlours.

Ideas and theories seemingly preposterous at the time have been propounded in these little bars on the tideway—and ventures, some glorious failures, others blazing the path to new countries, have resulted. Men have clambered down their slippery water-stairs and have sailed away, often to oblivion, but sometimes to become undying characters in our sea story; and those paradoxical features of the oceans, terror and peace, have perhaps come nearer explanation behind the round panes of their bow windows than anywhere else. Many have gone, dismissed either in kindly fashion by time or more abruptly by fire and high explosive, but too many remain for me to make more than a random selection in these notes.

Gravesend boasted more inns within throws of a waterman's heaving line than any other section of the Thames waterfront. West Street taverns, past and present, once had a reputation for lawlessness unrivalled in the history of the whole riverside; smugglers, cargo plunderers, crimps, dubious agents using the Dover Road, spies and wanted men frequented their bars. The few pubs that remain in this rambling water street are now over-shadowed by many years of dull respectability.

The oldest and most picturesque Gravesend tavern today is The Three Daws, licensed in the sixteenth century. It originally consisted of five cottages, probably dating from the end of the fifteenth century, which were converted by unemployed ship's carpenters, apparently unsupervised by an architect, for all windows and doors are of different sizes. Inside, the house is a labyrinth of passages and stairways. It was for this reason that the Admiralty issued a special order during the Napoleonic Wars whereby the Press Gang were to be reinforced when raiding The Three Daws as so many seamen escaped through its passages.

The bar is covered with a sheet of silver-pewter containing a higher percentage of silver than silver coinage. If its ancient walls could speak, they would tell of gentlemen adventurers and officers of caravels, East Indiamen, frigates, and clippers waiting for the tide, emigrants spending a last night in their native land, large-scale smuggling centred in its big cellars and, in later days, parties of Thames pilots awaiting their ships.

Another famous house remaining on the Gravesend water-front is The Clarendon. It was built in the eighteenth century as headquarters for the Lord High Admiral, then the Duke of York, who married the daughter of the Earl of Clarendon. It has an air of superiority, something of the grand manner, found in no other Thames-side tavern, obviously a survival of the days when royalty and other distinguished visitors slept under its roof. Its portico requires only a fall of snow and a waiting coach-and-four to provide a perfect setting for a traditional Christmas card.

At Tilbury, on the other side of the river, is The World's End, a rambling old pub on the edge of the marsh. Like not a few other features of Tilbury, it is popularly associated with Queen Elizabeth's historic review of her troops at the coming of the Armada, but there seems little evidence to substantiate the claim. It was at one time the residence of the Commanding Officer of Tilbury Fort, who, finding like many other Government servants in those times that his arrears of pay were unlikely to materialize, obtained a licence to convert it into the Fort Tavern*. Formerly the terminus

The Clarendon Hotel, Gravesend. Formerly the seventeenth-century home of Edward Hyde, Earl of Clarendon. King James II is believed to have stayed here.

of the Short Ferry to Gravesend, it was the rendezvous of the once ubiquitous Thames smuggler, Jacobites and Napoleonic spies.

The loneliest inn on Thames-side or, for that matter, in many other parts of the country, was Long Reach Tavern on the Dartford Marsh. It was in complete sympathy with the fen surrounding it, and its only neighbour was the post of the measured mile. About a century ago it was a noted centre for bare-knuckle prize fighting. The "fancy" who promoted the contests used to come down from London by wherry, and an adjacent meadow is still called "the fighting marsh".

When efforts were made to stop the bouts, it became customary to put sentries on the river wall, whence they commanded a good view of the surrounding lowlands; as a further precaution all plank bridges over strategic dykes in the vicinity were taken up. If the police did make a raid, the contestants, spectators and ring posts were bundled into skiffs and taken across the river to the Essex side, where the fight would be continued.

One noted fight at the Long Reach Tavern lasted all day. After a night's rest, the combatants resumed the struggle. After some hours the contest was stopped by a successful police raid. One of the fighters succeeded in escaping across the river, but the other ran into the tavern and dropped dead from exhaustion!*

At one time rivalling old Gravesend in the number of its hostelries were the banks of the Pool. Here were the taverns where the Elizabethan adventurers of London heard tales which sent them into the then unknown world and where succeeding generations of merchants and pioneers were in turn inspired to follow: the taverns where Shakespeare, Pepys, Defoe and others learnt to appreciate the beauty and perfection of seamen's speech.

The pressure of industry along the banks of the Pool has squeezed out many of the inns. However, most of those remaining are pubs of character. Most famous of the taverns on Pool-side or, for that matter, along the whole tideway, is The Prospect of Whitby on Wapping Wall. This old tavern is one of Thames's show places and attracts Mayfair and the curious from many lands as well as those few Thames watermen who survive. Its name derived from the once-thriving London–Yorkshire trade of coasting colliers; when the Prospect was built more than three centuries ago the Pool was sometimes filled to the point of congestion with the forerunners under sail of the big twentieth-century flatirons which carried on the trade until the decline in riverside gasworks and power stations halted London's largest import, coal.

*Told me by the late Frank C. Bowen, Gravesend historian.

*The old pub was destroyed by fire some time in the nineteenth-fifties.

The Prospect of Whitby at Wapping, formerly a typical waterman's pub, now a fashionable restaurant.
Photo: Stanley

There are two verandahs jutting over the tide on water-washed supports, and there is little doubt that many an illicit cargo was landed there in more lawless times. In one of the back rooms there are still the sockets for ring posts and supports for ringside seats, the only remaining relics of the prize fights that were fought there when the police had driven bare-knuckle fighting underground.

During our trip down river, we briefly looked at two other pubs in this area—The Turk's Head and The Town of Ramsgate. At Rotherhithe, on the south bank, is The Angel, which boasts the Captain's Room featured in Walter Besant's novel of that name. Nearby is The Mayflower, formerly The Spread Eagle and Crown. It was renamed because of its supposed association with the departure of the Pilgrim Fathers. Several London workmen joined the religious dissenters and they were said to have embarked here to join the *Mayflower*, awaiting them at Holehaven in the estuary.

Once the most notorious of London's sailortown pubs, but not actually on the waterfront, was The White Swan in the Highway at Wapping. Formerly the Ratcliffe Highway, the road was at one time the most evil in London. It consisted almost entirely of brothels, pubs of ill repute, gambling hells and lodging houses of the lowest types, all battening on the sailor with a big pay packet.

The worst of all these dens was The White Swan. The proprietor, an infamous Irish crimp and pimp, maintained that the stone swan on the roof was really a goose, and the pub was accordingly known as Paddy's Goose in the forecastles of the seven seas. Sexual shows were put on there not only for the benefit of drunken seamen but for Victorian noteables, including, it was said, royalty.

After the war, the old pub and its adjoining hall, both long derelict, were pulled down. By then, Ratcliffe Highway, renamed the Highway, had left its past behind; today it features prominently in Dockland development.

Among taverns destroyed during the blitz was The Dog and Duck at the head of the old Rotherhithe watermen's stairs of that name. It could be reached only by a footpath said to have been in use for more than three centuries. The name derived from a cruel sport whereby water spaniels chased pinioned wild duck, which tried to escape by repeated diving.

The rebuilt Yacht at Greenwich is now renowned more for the quality of its food than the watermen's yarns once heard at its bars. Neighbouring it is the bow-windowed Trafalgar. For some time it lay derelict before being turned into flats, but after the war it resumed its role as a Thames-side hostelry. It was either here or at the nearby Ship Inn that Lord Palmerston once contemplated a dish of whitebait and said to his companions: "Let us all imitate this wise little fish, and drink a lot and say nothing."*

The old unspoiled pub in Narrow Street, Limehouse, The Grapes, rivals The Prospect of Whitby as being the prototype of Dickens's Six Jolly Fellowship Porters in *Our Mutual Friend*. But 98 Narrow Street (formerly part of Sparks's establishment), which was once The Two Brewers, was, according to George F. Young (writing in *The Dickensian* in 1935) the most likely to have inspired Dickens. A pleasant watercolour formerly in the Port of London Authority's collection showed The Two Brewers built out over the river on a crazy-looking wooden structure, but the riverward part of the premises had long since disappeared.

At the abandoned Royal Docks are three hotel/pubs, the Connaught, Central Buffet and The Galleons, all likely to be preserved. The Connaught neighbours a unique cast-iron urinal,

Scrap Book of London River by A. G. Thompson (Bradley, 1937).

The Trafalgar Hotel, Greenwich. Gladstone and other ministers of the Crown used to come here by river for celebrated whitebait dinners in the Nelson Room.

to be preserved with the hotel! It overlooks a once favourite spot where dissident dockers were harangued by their leaders.

In the outskirts of Tilbury Docks was the solidly comfortable Victorian Tilbury Hotel, built by the old dock company and bequeathed to the PLA. It was designed for a more leisurely age when communications were such that passengers and their friends often stayed overnight at Tilbury so as to be ready for an early morning embarkation or arrival. A landmark to passing rivermen, it was something of a white elephant to the PLA. Nevertheless, it had a small regular clientele who were attracted by the unrivalled panorama of ships in Gravesend Reach, which they could watch through the telescope mounted in the lounge. The hotel was built of timber and made a sadly spectacular bonfire in 1944 when it was completely destroyed by incendiary bombs.

This brief review of some tideway pubs deals only with those east of London Bridge; this focal point separates London River from the River of London. Although, say, The London Apprentice at Isleworth, with its tales of highwaymen, The Doves at Hammersmith, where James Thomson began The Seasons, or The Bull's Head at Strand-on-the-Green, where Cromwell sojourned, also have an appealing past and a tidewater frontage, their traditions are more those of what may be called the London Londoner than those of the seafaring Londoner.

But, upstream or down, all the older tideway pubs have been council chambers of Father Thames, and not a little of his glorious tale has been told in their venerable bars and parlours.

Greenwich 7

IT WAS in the nineteen-fifties, before the world's far places became so much nearer for holidaymakers, that I was frequently asked where the finest backcloth to tidal Thames was to be found. Like most experts when asked for an authoritative opinion, I generally hedged, replying that it depended upon time and weather. And I had to admit that the river reach which looked magnificently tragic at flood tide and under a westering sun often seemed to shrink to a stagnant puddle with low tide and the sun in a different quarter. Also I was human enough to enjoy explaining at some length that this building needed a bonnet of storm clouds to set it off, that one bore inspection only as a silhouette, that another needed a mask of steamer smoke to hide its ravaged features, and so on.

When, however, I sensed that patience was running out, I gave my considered opinion that one of the few Thames vistas which never completely lost their beauty whatever the tide or sun, was the Royal Naval College at Greenwich. Significant of a day when the tideway was London's main passenger thoroughfare, it presents its best elevation to the river; but to appreciate it to the full, it should be approached from upstream. When the voyager comes round the river bend from Limehouse Reach into Greenwich Reach the majestic scene is enhanced by the gracious river curve. I have admired this view countless times in the course of my journeyings up and down the Thames, and more than once I have dined in the Painted Hall, probably the finest service mess in the world.

Harking back to the nineteen-fifties, I was then permitted by courtesy of the College authorities to go behind the curtain of Naval tradition and inspect in some detail what had become the University of the Silent Service. Like many successful British institutions, Greenwich Naval College is an adaptation. It was begun by Charles II in 1664 as a royal dwelling on the site of the Palace of Placentia, the favourite residence of the Tudors. The architect was John Webb, a nephew of Inigo Jones. A start was made on only one block of the King's House in Charles's reign, but after one wing had been completed the project lay dormant for more than twenty years. When William and Mary ascended the throne, the Queen decided to found at Greenwich a hospital for necessitous seamen of the Royal Navy, and the Royal Hospital at Greenwich was promoted under Royal Charter on 25th October, 1694.

Sir Christopher Wren, who was commissioned to carry out the work, proposed to demolish the remains of the old palace as well as the unfinished King's House and the beautiful little Queen's House where part of the National Maritime Museum is now housed. But the Queen refused to allow the destruction of the two houses and insisted on an uninterrupted vista, 115 feet wide, from the Queen's House to the river. Wren's second design was accepted; this required the river bank to be straightened to provide a base for a building symmetrical with the existing wing of the King's House. To further this part of his plan, he tipped the ruins of the old palace into the river. The buildings were finally completed in 1758, first under the supervision of Wren and then, after his death in 1716, of various eminent architects. With only minor changes, the blocks remain as they were built.

The first pensioners took up residence in the hospital in 1705 and indigent seamen were maintained there until 1869. In 1873, the pensioners by then having been so reduced in numbers that they had been granted larger pensions and sent home, the Royal Naval College moved to Greenwich from Portsmouth.

The infirmary, built to accommodate unfit pensioners, was made over to the Merchant Navy in 1873; it became the Dreadnought Hospital, thus retaining the name of a hulk in the Thames off Greenwich, which had hitherto provided for incapacitated merchant seamen. The Royal Hospital School for children of the pensioners migrated from Greenwich to new quarters at Holbrook, Suffolk, in 1933.

The King Charles block, the oldest part of the establishment, was damaged by enemy action, but most of the destruction was mercifully hidden from the river. It was here that Pepys worked during the flight from the Great Plague. One wonders if the saviour of the Navy was conscious that, on the site of a former palace where the Queen was saluted by Drake after his circumnavigation of the globe, he, the little Clerk of the Acts, was also making British maritime history. And was it with pretty Nellie, or some other naughty lovely, in view that Charles caused two secret doors, cunningly disguised as bookcases and difficult to discern, to be constructed in what became part of the College offices? But I felt that the handsome, hand-carved mantelpiece that graced the same room was rather severe for the fireside dalliance which prudish Victorian historians would have us believe was the principal activity of the Merry Monarch.

In the King William building, the first planned by Wren to be completed, is the gem of the College, the Painted Hall. It was originally intended to be the refectory of the pensioners, the upper chamber for the officers and the lower for the pensioners, but it was not long used for that purpose. Sir James Thornhill contracted

to paint the walls and ceiling at £3 per square yard for the ceiling and at £1 per square yard for the walls, a task which he began in 1708. It was not long before he realized that his tender was absurdly low and he pleaded for an increase in the rate of pay. But the hospital commissioners insisted on their pound of paint and he was paid no more than the stipulated sum, £6,685 for nineteen years' work.

The ceiling is painted in the baroque style and the pictures show little restraint in their portrayal of royalty: King William and Queen Mary are attended by the four cardinal virtues; in addition love, peace, liberty, time, truth, architecture, fame, wisdom and heroic virtue are attendant on the throne, while tyranny, ambition, envy, covetousness, detraction, calumny and other vices are all discomforted by the royal paragons. Ships, rivers, coats of arms, the arts and sciences, old philosophers, and Flamsteed, the first Astronomer Royal, all merge into a breath-taking picture.

In the centre of the ceiling of the upper hall are represented

The Royal Naval College, Greenwich, one of the architectural gems of the tidal Thames.
Photo: Stanley

69

Queen Anne and Prince George of Denmark accompanied by a number of emblematical figures. On the south and north walls respectively are paintings of the landing of the Prince of Orange at Brixham and the landing of King George I at Greenwich. On the wall facing the entrance are portraits of George I and two generations of his family surrounded by tutelary virtues which, if Thackeray is to be believed, were not usually found in that royal presence. In the lower right-hand corner Sir James Thornhill has added a self portrait and it is perhaps not without significance that he shows himself holding out his hand.

The Painted Hall is a beautiful and impressive room enhanced by the magnificent old tables at which some five hundred people can be seated. To see it on guest night is to witness some of the dignity and ceremony of a gracious and colourful era which has almost passed elsewhere. But the thing which impressed me most in the Painted Hall or, indeed, in the whole of the college, might well pass unnoticed by the uninformed visitor. Let into the stone floor near the entrance is a tablet dated 15th June, 1941, which declares: "On this day came three citizens of the United States of America, the first of their countrymen to become sea officers of the Royal Navy." The Limeys' "Thank you"!

The chapel in the Queen Mary building has the pious maturity of the age in which it was built. It was part of the Royal Hospital and was completed to the design of Wren in 1752. In 1779 much of it was destroyed by fire. It was restored by James Stuart, Surveyor of the Hospital, and reopened in 1789. The chapel portal, consisting of an architrave, frieze and cornice of statutary marble and with great folding doors of elaborately carved mahogany, is one of the finest church entrances in the country. Despite the general simplicity, there is much to admire inside the chapel, particularly paintings in chiaroscuro of the Apostles and Evangelists by an Italian artist, Biagio Rebecca, and a painting by Sir Benjamin West of the preservation of St Paul and his companions from shipwreck on Malta.

The circular pulpit is supported by six fluted columns and is richly carved. Much of it is believed to have been the work of naval shipwrights from the former Royal Dockyards at Woolwich and Deptford, and the craftsmanship combined with the mellow beauty of old wood is one of the sights of the College. The chapel contains some fine silver-gilt communion plate; one chalice dated 1507 probably belonged to the chapel of the Palace of Placentia. The lectern and the wooden font are those originally supplied to the chapel; they were lost for some years but eventually found in the dome and, after restoration, were brought back into use in 1935.

In the Queen Anne building is a small crypt which is all that remains of the old palace. The pattern of the brickwork in the crypt is somewhat similar to that in the former Crescent Wine Vaults at the London Docks, but the narrow Tudor bricks show its greater age. Lying in the crypt when I visited it were some ancient wooden drainpipes discovered during excavations in the College premises, and ranged against the wall were several superannuated gargoyles.

It must not be supposed that the Royal Naval College is merely a museum. It contains some workmanlike laboratories and classrooms where officers of all ranks from sub-lieutenant to rear-admiral attend as students for periods varying from six months to three years. Nearly every executive officer and many other commissioned officers pass through the College at some time in their naval careers. The techniques of modern sea warfare could possibly be as well taught in a dozen other places in the British Isles, as the wartime temporary training depots proved. But it would be hard to find a more suitable place for teaching all-important naval tradition. Built on the site of the royal palace from which Elizabeth I watched her ships and gentlemen adventurers going down to the sea, still reverencing the room where Nelson's body lay in state after Trafalgar, Greenwich Naval College has become the heart of the Navy. It has had a long and close affinity with the London tideway on which it stands, and the royal river boasts no fairer jewel in its crown.

Behind the College stands the National Maritime Museum. In the nineteen-fifties, before the tragic decline in British sea power, I found the country's long sea story, written in the blood of many generations, told with admirable continuity; here the very essence of maritime triumphs and disasters, distilled in the retort of time, had crystallised into an inspiration.

The Museum was established by Act of Parliament in 1930 for the illustration and study of the maritime history of Great Britain. The Trustees have interpreted the subject in its widest sense as comprehending the activities of the Royal Navy, the Merchant Service and the fishing fleet, together with all that throws light on the lives and work of all seamen. The Museum is housed mainly in the buildings vacated in 1932 by the Royal Hospital School. But the outstanding building of the group is the beautiful Queen's House designed by Inigo Jones in 1618 for Anne of Denmark. This little palace bridged the original Deptford–Woolwich road which then ran through the house, and it was probably the first dwelling-place of modern compactness to be erected in this country.

The Museum has no more than friendly relations with the adjacent Royal Naval College, and its administration, so often confused with that of the College, is quite distinct. Its facilities for students are exceptionally good, while the general public appreciates its modern display methods and excellent restaurant.

However, in keeping with this record of Thames memories, I must return to the visit I made in the nineteen-fifties. The galleries were nearly all arranged in periods, and one could walk with our greatest seamen of all ages, inspect our historic ships and fight again our decisive sea battles. Despite the average of five hundred visitors a day (nearly trebled by 1990) and notwithstanding the post-war shortage of staff, the rooms and galleries were maintained with the order and scrupulous cleanliness found elsewhere in HM Ships of that period. Not that this was a matter for wonder, for the Director, Lieutenant-Commander F. G. G. Carr, RNVR, well known as a nautical writer and yachtsman, had assistant curators every whit as keen as himself, and the general staff were Royal Naval and Royal Marine pensioners to a man.

You are to imagine, then, stately and lofty galleries where ship models, pictures, navigational instruments of all ages, ancient charts, historic documents, terrestrial globes, sculptures, nautical books, medals, seals and personal relics of great seamen were displayed and explained. Nelson and Cook have left such a wealth of relics that they were assigned special galleries. Ship's time was kept in the Museum, and measured strokes on the bell of HMS *Vanguard*, Nelson's flagship at the battle of the Nile, mounted in a belfry made from timbers of famous ships, struck the half hours. It is, of course, impossible within the scope of this record to write about more than a fraction of the Museum's almost countless treasures, and I can mention only briefly those exhibits of particular appeal to a devoted Thamesman.

The ship models were nearly all contemporary dockyard models. An exception was a beautiful little model of the 60-gun *Centurion* of 1732, in which Anson made his voyage round the world; this was Anson's own model. An interesting sidelight on the models was that excessive gilding, the encircling of ports with gilded wreaths and other gingerbread work, ceased by Admiralty order in 1703. This order was a clear line of demarcation in warship design and helped modern curators to date models of doubtful vintage.

The model of another old-timer was the Deptford ship *Royal George*, sunk with Kempenfelt at Spithead in 1782 and the subject of Cowper's ode *Toll for the Brave*. Not that all the models were of the long past. In Neptune's Hall was a wealth of later models including *Cleopatra*, which brought the famous Needle to the Thames, models of old and new types of light vessels, a model of Conrad's lovely little *Torrens* and models of many modern warships and merchantmen then well known in the Port of London. A particular treasure was a large-scale model of the gallant and immortal P&O liner *Rawalpindi*. As a Thamesman, I was much interested in a diorama of the loss of the *Princess Alice*, sunk in the tideway in 1878.

But to me the pictures and prints were the chief glory of the Museum. Here were Drake, Frobisher, Nelson, Howe, Cook and many other famous seamen looking gravely down at us from the past. Here were enormous canvases of sea battles as decisive to our todays as the Battle of Britain will be to our grandchildren. Other pictures portrayed in bloody detail almost unremembered duels between rival ships and attacks on places whose very names have been almost forgotten. But each picture was the blueprint of a course in the arch of British sea power in its heyday. Battles with the sea itself, the seaman's oldest enemy, were the subject of other pictures. Many famous ships, stepping stones in the climb of human progress, were pictured in all their panoply of sail, colour, pennants and rope tracery.

The Thames flows through many of the pictures. Blackwall, Deptford, Woolwich and Greenwich, with their ships and flags and pageantry of great occasions, appeared in many media. Several pictures were from the brush of John Cleveley the Elder, an eighteenth-century matey in Deptford Dockyard who turned professional artist. Many others were painted by Van de Velde the Younger, who painted scenes of war in the time of Charles II.

With a last glance at the magnificent Hogarth, *Lord George Graham in his Cabin*, we must beat up for the Navigation Room. Here I found a detailed record of the seaman's preoccupation with time and place throughout the centuries. His early efforts to signpost the stars were confused by the intrusion of astrology, as evidenced by astrological signs incorporated in certain early astrolabes. Drake's astrolabe was one of this room's greatest treasures. Here I was shown Harrison's chronometers, one of which was the winning entry for the Government prize of £20,000. In the same room were some of the hour glasses, or rather, half-hour glasses, on which earlier seamen had to rely.

Among early charts in the Navigation Room were two of the Thames Estuary by John Thornton, who made them in 1682; for a cartographer with no conception of modern surveying methods, at first glance they seemed reasonably accurate.

In the Medal Room an ingenious system of lighting and mirrors enabled visitors to see both obverse and reverse of the exhibits. Some of the medals, in particular the Dutch medals commemorating the raid up the Medway, are nearly as large as small saucers. The Atlantic Telegraph Cable Medal, struck when the *Great Eastern* had completed her only useful job of work in 1866, appropriately bears the arms of Great Britain and the United States.

In the nineteen-fifties there were some ten thousand volumes in the Library several of them above price. Ancient atlases, famous logs and collections of personal papers of many eminent seamen inspire imagination.

Documents of more modern history were on show in Neptune's Hall. Among them was Hitler's fateful order of 31st August, 1939, to begin war on Poland. In the adjacent translation the blunt phrase: "I have decided upon a solution by force" focused the imagination on how it all began. In this hall Prien's log of *U 47*, recording the undersea attack that sank the *Royal Oak* in Scapa Flow in October, 1939, was also displayed.

Scores of other exhibits of interest to Thames-side were on show when I first visited the Museum. Since then, many new features attractively displayed by modern methods have been added. But in the nineteen-fifties, river traffic still streamed past Greenwich on every tide and the collection was then an inspiration to the greatest seafaring nation the world had ever known.

Cutty Sark in her permanent dry berth on the Greenwich waterfront.
Courtesy: Cutty Sark Maritime Trust

River Men   8

THE tidal Thames has been aptly described as our "Island line of life and fate", and, indeed, its waters have run like a mighty and recurrent theme through much of the nation's story. Always in the background of the tideway's long tale have been the people of the river—individualistic, tenacious, clannish and skilful, philosophers all; and only by their unflagging service have the kings and princes, statesmen, colonists, merchants and seamen voyaged out and home on the robust tides. For centuries these men of the Thames changed but little, for their traditions were inspired by the unchanging and ageless river. But, since the nineteen-fifties, both men and river have changed as never before for hundreds of years.

Labour unrest that has occurred along the Thames from time to time has been a part of the river pattern, for daily contact with ships and tides and other elemental things has always engendered an unrestful spirit. Through the ages rulers and prelates, law and authority, HM Customs and the Admiralty Press Gang have encountered resistance in making these men conform to the ways of the shore.

After the last war, despite these labour troubles, civic pride was high, for the riverman evinced an almost proprietorial pride in the fine ships then using the Thames and glimpsed something of the great heritage behind the ceaseless coming and going of commerce. It was particularly those who were the most receptive of the dripping venom of the professional agitator who usually most hotly contested any aspersions on London's pre-eminence as a port. There, perhaps, lies the antidote to unrest in other industries, and we may find it politic to foster this local pride instead of attempting the standardization which blights so much that once flourished.

A hundred years ago, Mayhew wrote: "The dock labourers (of London) are a striking instance of mere brute force with brute appetites. This class of labour is as unskilled as the power of the hurricane." But by the nineteen-fifties times had indeed changed, for, although the man with the hand truck still performed much useful work in the service of cargo distribution, the machine was playing an ever more important part alongside the ship. Today technology has taken off from those times and both ships and cargo handling bear little resemblance to those of the immediate post-war years.

The belief, handed down like so many other outworn creeds

from the excesses accompanying the Industrial Revolution, that machines usher in grim distress dies hard. It is true that a great number of dockers have been replaced by machines, but they were elderly workers, nearing pensionable age, and redundancy pay has been extremely generous. Those who remain take pride in the novel machines now handling cargo—complicated machines needing skill and judgment. And only three or four decades ago, the men now using them would have qualified for Mayhew's devastating description.

Much the same trend is noticeable in the river, where the one-time shovel engineers of the steam tugs in the nineteen-fifties now serve the diesel engine. Voith-Schneider propulsion and other innovations have completely revolutionized ship-towage in the Thames. And the greatly reduced number of lightermen have metaphorically followed the legendary mariner in casting away their oars, not with the same objective of retirement far from the sea, but because they now mostly voyage without effort behind a panting craft tug.

Despite, or perhaps due to, the influence of the BBC, dockland speech has seriously degenerated in colour and imagination. The rounded, gusty, all-embracing oaths of other days were replaced in the post-war period by the monotonous single word used as noun, adjective and verb. Native Cockney, too, began to wilt in the nineteen-fifties under the weight of imported Transatlantic idiom, some of it introduced during the American occupation of Dockland for the D-Day build-up and confirmed by imported television entertainment. The resultant hybrid colloquialisms of the younger Thames-siders have been mainly gibberish, not very intelligible either to the Old or the New World. Nevertheless, the more difficult names of some of the ships using the port continue to be mangled as fearfully as ever, and shipowners might well consider what their selections from the classics may degenerate into on the lips of untutored dockers.

Some thirty years ago tideway fashions began to undergo subtle modifications. The bowler hat, for instance, now almost extinct, began to disappear. Up to the nineteen-forties this very English headgear was the undress uniform hat of authority and was donned almost as a rite by dock pilots, tugmasters, foremen and others whose orders were obeyed by the be-capped lower strata of riverine society. Perhaps its significance weakened during the period when caste was expunged by the ubiquitous tin helmet. Whatever the reason, the head once crowned by the bowler now looks safer under the protective plastic helmet.

For some time after the war khaki battle-dress was almost *de rigueur* in lighters and tugs and on the wharves and quays, but the wartime issue soon wore out. For a time the former shabby

nondescript garments came back, and then boiler suits and other more suitable clothing began to come in. I fear I shall never see again the elderly barge master who, in the early twenties, passed me in the Lower Hope at the helm of his craft; he was wearing a decayed frock coat, a cloth cap with ear flaps and sea boots.

The Thames has always been a true mirror of the seas, faithfully reflecting changes sweeping the outer world. Some old methods and traditional customs still need to be changed, and there are grievous results of changing too fast and too far. But nowhere in the crowded mirror is to be seen the shadow of despair.

Practically all the river men are more or less exposed to the weather; in the old days, they were, by contemporary standards, poorly paid, and few had security of employment. In spite of, or because of, these drawbacks, robust tideway humour was plentiful. Before the war it was usually bucolic slapstick fun, but radio and television have brought about a subtle change, for there is now a taste for the wisecrack instead of the custard pie.

I have already repeated some of the scurrilous stories about Thames pilots. Another equally improbable yarn concerns a pilot who, steaming too fast in a thick fog, asked his waterman stationed on the forecastle head if he could see anything. He replied that he was close to two ships and that he was bound to hit one of them. "What looks the cheaper?" asked the pilot. And on being told that there was a deep-sea ship to starboard and only a coaster to port, he ordered "Hard a-port."

A true story concerns the skipper (long retired) of one of the former LCC penny steamboats. He was ordered to discharge the mate for being habitually drunk. When the mate was paid off, he gave the skipper a receipt in the form of a mighty punch on the jaw. In his own words, the skipper went on: "When I came round I found myself in hospital with a doctor and a lot of students round my bed. The doctor was saying: 'Now this case was caused by a —', and he rattled out a Latin name as long as Woolwich Reach. So I sat up and said: 'You're wrong, guv'nor. It was caused by a blee'n punch on the jaw.'"

Another true story was told to me by a PLA diver. He had to take a load of diving equipment across London during a rush hour. The driver of the van was a Cockney youth and the diver said he would never forget that ride. Almost every road rule was broken, appalling risks were taken, and the youth revealed himself as the world's worst driver. When they reached their destination, the driver remarked to the nerve-shattered diver: "I suppose your job's pretty dangerous."

Portable bits of cargo were a constant temptation to men living impoverished and insecure existences. HM Customs once supervised the pouring of contraband wine down a drain. They did not know that red ink and water were being destroyed and that every jug, jar, mug and pail in the warehouse contained wine. On another occasion, I saw with pity a hunchback making for the dock gate. There a PLA policeman stopped him and expertly withdrew a leg of frozen lamb—the hunch—from beneath his coat.

From the PLA police I had the story of George. He was helping to discharge a cargo of whisky, thinking all the time it was a sin to expose such a cargo to the perils of sea carriage. When work ended and he came ashore, a detective observed that George frequently clapped his hand to his heart as if suffering from remorse or heartburn. The detective stopped him, inquired after his health and caused him to be searched. Under his coat, nestling against his heart, was a bottle containing a liquid that looked and smelt like whisky. George's feelings were hurt. He stiffly explained that it was medicine for his son. He alleged that he had collected it on his way to work and that it had been in the pocket of his jacket, which had been hanging in the ship's hold all day. But a test proved that the liquid was in fact whisky.

George was game to the last. At the Court next day he said he was completely puzzled how the medicine could have been changed into whisky. The magistrate replied that there was only one recorded case in which water had been changed into wine, and that was regarded as a miracle. George hopefully: "If it happened once, it could happen again." Magistrate: "Two months' hard labour."

Even at fortune's lowest ebb, the people of the river maintained the blunt independence which has been and continues to be one of their chief characteristics. Before the war, before the days of industrial canteens, most dockers carried their lunch clapped between two plates tied in a bandanna. Once I inadvertently sat on such a packet. At the sound of splintering china I sprang up. The elderly docker who owned it gathered together the broken fragments in the bandanna without a word. "I'm fearfully sorry", I ventured. He made no reply and I repeated my apology. Then he took his pipe out of his mouth and spoke in measured tones. "If I", he said, "had a bloody canary as pretty as you and I wrung its blee'n neck, saying I was sorry wouldn't bring the poor little bugger back to life again." He said no more, ignoring my offers of compensation.

The varied British and foreign uniforms which had lent so much colour to dockland during the war soon faded from the memory of the public. Not that the public was ever very knowledgeable about such things. I well remember the rage of a senior naval officer during the war when he was taken for a commissionaire at a London store. One of the PLA Harbour-masters told me of a somewhat similar experience. These men wear a slight variation of Merchant Navy officers' uniform. Going off duty late one night, he sat in a bus beside another passenger who gratuitously informed him that it was very cold and that his daily work exposed him to this inclement weather. Whereupon the Harbourmaster mentioned mildly that he, too, found his working conditions taxing. The other passenger looked respectfully at his uniform and replied: "Yes. I dunno how you chaps stand the way the wind sweeps round them platforms every time a train comes in."

Before the last great war, over seven thousand Thames lighters were in daily use; their total capacity was more than a million tons (tonnes). They rendered an invaluable service transporting cargo from ship to riverside warehouse, from industry to ship, from deep-sea ship to transshipment vessel and so on. All told, they distributed about ninety per cent of London's imports.

Many were still wooden craft, but steel barges were increasing. It was these, and the damage they might do when coming alongside, that caused several spritsail barges to keep a dog on board (a pedigree Medway barge hound was the description of one such mongrel). All Thames barges were swim-headed—with bluff bows sloping inward—ending in a budget—a sort of fixed rudder. Apart from special craft, they ranged in capacity from fifty tons to 750 tons (for grain). The most popular size loaded 160 tons.

The container revolution in cargo transport has virtually killed the Thames lighterage trade. The few barges now in use are usually towed by craft tugs, but up to the last war many of them, especially those belonging to the smaller lighterage firms, were each driven by a solitary lighterman. With the aid of his oars, twenty feet long, he would row his laden barge upstream or down, taking advantage of every eddy and set of tidal currents. Lightermen and watermen of the Thames are highly skilled workers who serve a seven-year apprenticeship before becoming Freemen of their ancient guild, the 400-year-old Company of Watermen and Lightermen of the River Thames. In the days when headgear labelled status, most of these men wore a bowler hat to signify professional standing.

They were completely exposed to weather. When barges were nearly all driven, they might take their craft from, say, Rotherhithe to Tilbury, a passage of more than twenty miles, perhaps using the motive power of two successive ebb tides. The lighterman's greatest fear was of being marooned by fog and thus being unable to get ashore. The only shelter was a cubby hole aft, equipped with a small stove but rarely with any fuel, and they usually had only sufficient rations for the passage. An extra day or two under these conditions meant real hardship.

These men were mainly responsible for the grapevine that passed news up and down the tideway. One story tells of two lightermen in passing craft. As they drew level one asked the other how his wife was. As they began to draw apart the lady was reported quite well. Still further apart, the first man bawled: "If I tell you something, promise to keep it to yourself." By this time they were only just within hailing distance. On receiving the assurance, he roared: "Well Liz is in the family way again."

Most picturesque of pre-war craft were the spritsail barges. Their red sails, lee-boards and mizzen sheeted to the rudder head were unique. Manned by only two men, they were to be seen in the docks, in the main river, in the estuary swatchways and up tidal creeks shallow enough to be waded. Most were of wood although some steel coasting barges had been built. The average length was about eighty feet with a beam of some eighteen feet. Flat bottomed, they had a very shallow draught. "Sail 'em in a heavy dew," claimed the enthusiasts. Indeed, one yarn tells of the mate being knocked overboard by the sail; he picked himself up and, it is alleged, *ran* after his craft. In the Thames, these men were known as sailormen.

Thames spritsail barges. Once a familiar sight on the lower river reaches, they have almost completely vanished.
Photo: Stanley

These sailing barges belonged to well-defined types. There were stumpies, without a topsail and largely employed in the carriage of bricks; hay barges, their loads piled more than ten feet above the deck and the mate perched on top of the stack acting as lookout for the skipper at the wheel; and a few boomies with boom-rigged mainsails instead of the more usual spritsails.

A Rochester barge usually brought a loud "baa" from passing craft on the strength of a legend that a Rochester barge hand had, long ago, been hanged for sheep stealing.

Apart from special fleets such as the formerly famous Blue Circle cement barges, these sailing craft were virtually tramps, seeking freights such as flour, grain, coal, timber and explosives when and where opportunity offered. The crew of two were usually on shares and when trade was bad had to subsist on subs from the owner, to be paid back when they were earning again. Barges temporarily idle often tied up at Woolwich Buoys, known for this reason as Starvation Buoys. Under sail alone, these craft have vanished.

Since early days when the ancients recorded the known and imaginary horrors likely to beset travellers, maps and charts have interested even the stay-at-homes. The navigation chart is the cream of such records, for in addition to delineating coasts and waterways, landmarks, watermarks, shoals and wrecks, it deals with a second dimension, depth. The accuracy of British charts is accepted the world over; the reason for their high standard is found in the Admiralty *Manual of Hydrographic Surveying*, which, after setting out the many professional qualifications the successful marine surveyor must acquire, adds: "The principal qualification of an efficient surveyor is an unlimited capacity for taking pains and conscientious devotion to accuracy of detail in his work, coupled with a methodical and orderly mind."

Bearing all this in mind and with memories of spotty vision resulting from anxious study of the figures recording low-water depths, I spent a day out in the late nineteen-fifties with the Port of London Authority's Marine Survey Service. The senior officer told me that the section for which he was responsible stretched from Erith to the then seaward limit of the Port. He and his assistants had to keep a continuous check on the ever-changing contours of the river bed, regularly supplying soundings and other relevant information to the PLA as well as to Admiralty cartographers.

They obtained records of wreck and other obstruction for the Harbour and Salvage Services, positioned dredgers and screwing lighters (used for screwing moorings into the river bed), co-operated with Trinity House by reporting the position of navigational buoys, positioned public and private moorings, and, in

fact, performed duties of precision afloat and ashore needing the use of surveying instruments and calling for the qualifications laid down in the admiralty Manual. Casting the lead had already given way to the Echo-sounder. At the time of my visit, they were testing a recent modern addition—the Decca Navigator. This system uses radio position lines transmitted in the form of a grid from Decca transmitting stations. This seemed to me to be as near push-button navigation as humanity could devise, but I have no doubt that major developments have since taken place and will continue to occur.

We prepared to take soundings near the Chapman Light. Accuracy was the most important feature of the plan. An inaccurate report of the depth of the Yantlet Channel might either imperil ships or unnecessarily set in motion highly expensive dredging operations. Accordingly, two suitable landmarks were selected and the angles from the starting point laid out on the chart. The ship's boat went off with one of the crew equipped with a synchronized watch. He was landed on the Chapman Light ready to take readings of the tide gauge at five-minute intervals.

When the boat returned, it was anchored at the landward end of the soundings run, its position checked by sextant and Decca Navigator. Then the ship moved out to the seaward end of the run.

The PLA survey launch Chartwell. *Many hours of careful work are necessary to provide the Thames navigational charts.*

Again, our position was checked meticulously. Then with the signal hoist "ONE" (engaged in surveying operations) at the halyard peak, we turned and ran back over the course. The ship's position in relation to the selected landmarks was checked every two degrees of angle and at the same time the graph of the echo sounder was marked by remote control. As we ran in, our course was checked by sextant from the anchored boat. As I watched the hairbreadth steering of the helmsman, team work by the surveying officers, the boat's crew waiting at the end of our run and the tide watcher on the Chapman, I felt they combined to provide a lesson which might be copied with advantage by the Ship of State.

I was later informed that all I had seen was only preparatory to many hours of work in their plotting room. The term backroom boys is now out of date, but it is the description that best fits Thames Marine Surveyors. Few of the people of the river, even seafarers, know the meaning of the flag hoist "ONE" without reference to the code book. Quietly and unobtrusively, these architects of the tideway probe the deeps and shallows, as much exposed to weather as the seamen, but without the satisfaction of completing a voyage, for theirs is a true labour of Sisyphus. Their work will never finish while tidal shoals grow, shift and disperse. Countless lives and cargoes pass in and out of the port in safety by their courtesy.

Dockmasters are all marooned master mariners. They were (in the Port of London dock groups now closed) and are (at Tilbury Docks) responsible for co-ordinating all movement afloat in the vast lagoons, for the passage of ships (called stemming) into and out of dry docks, and for the swinging or lifting of all dock road bridges. And the crux of their work centred on the locks, the vital water gates of the docks. For instance, before the Royal Docks were closed, some three thousand ships and over thirty thousand barges passed through their locks each year.

Most Port of London docks are impounded by pumps to a level of two and a half feet above average high water in the river outside. As Thames tides rise and fall some twenty feet, locks are virtually gigantic lifts to raise ships up to the level of dock water or down to the river.

Again taking the now defunct Royal Docks as an example, the King George V Lock is (still) 800 feet long and 100 feet wide. When the rising tide had given sufficient depth of water over the lock cill, the blue docking flag would be hoisted to signify that it was ready to receive customers (all previously booked by telephone in the dockmaster's lockside office). Two tugs would deftly position the ship in the river and hold her there against the tide while a waterman's skiff ferried a head rope ashore. From then on the dockmaster was in sole charge, conducting all manoeuvres by the pipe of his whistle and hand signals.

Under its own power, the ship would slowly enter the lock, one of the tugs hanging on to her tail to hold her against the sweep of tide across the entrance. To the landsman it would seem like an attempt to put the proverbial quart into a pint pot, but, even with a gale blowing, the dockmaster would be mortified if the ship touched while moving into the lock.

The dockmaster would walk backwards watching the incoming ship, with remote control of the engines and whistle signals to his own locking crew who marched slowly beside the moving ship carrying huge check ropes. These ropes would be whipped on or off hydraulic capstans or bollards as directed. A series of chirrups by the dockmaster would indicate that the ship was in position and could be made fast. More whistles, and the lock gates would be shut and the sluices opened to allow the lock to fill to the level of the dock water.

The ship's bridge and boat deck, only a few feet above the lock side, would rise slowly until, some thirty minutes later, the vessel would tower over the lock walls. At this point the Trinity House (Mud) pilot would hand over to the dock pilot.

The whistle would at last bring attention back to the ship. The road bridge would be swung, the inner lock gates opened, and

A ship entering a dock lock. The PLA Dockmaster controls the ship's engines, with whistle signals to his crew.

85

dock tugs would back in and make fast. A last whistle, and the ship would move slowly out of the lock to take up her allotted berth in the dock. It would all be done as smoothly as a hand sliding into a silk glove. And, perhaps typically British, the whole operation would have been conducted without a single shouted order. Once, long before air travellers could week-end in far places, I was enormously impressed by a dockmaster's cavalier treatment of outwardbound romance. As a ship moved out into the river, he waved to the master on the ship's bridge and gave him a casual "so long" as if he were seeing a friend off on a bus ride.

I do not know if stevedores play any part in the stuffing of containers in modern sea carriage, but in the case of old-fashioned break-bulk vessels, in which the stowage of cargo has altered little since Phoenician ships carried Cornish tin, the work of the stevedore is all-important.

The ship, having discharged inward freight, is ready to receive export cargo. Under the watching eye of the Cargo Superintendent, who has prepared a stowage plan whereby the first cargo out will be the last in the hold (otherwise a gigantic game of Hunt the Slipper would be necessary at each port of call) the stevedores will stow the cargo. They know better than to put a steam roller on top

Container operation No 40 berth, Tilbury Docks.

86

of crates of eggs, but other matters must also be considered. Sometimes weighty cases must be put high up in the hold and low down in others to ensure that the ship will roll smoothly in a seaway and not jerk and so strain the structure. Again, the weight must be distributed throughout the length of the ship so that she will not be down by the head with the propeller half out of the water, or down by the stern with the bows in the air. And despite the Superintendent's careful preparations, an urgent unexpected piece may turn up only hours before the ship is due to sail.

A monitor of all this activity is the Plimsoll Disc or the ship's marks on the hull. It consists of a circle with a line across the centre which is the summer standard above which the vessel may not be submerged. Above it are two more lines indicating the safety limit in a tropical zone and that in fresh water. This monitor takes its name from Samuel Plimsoll, who fought for the introduction of these safety measures in the bad old days of criminal overloading.

I once saw a flock of sheep milling about on a dock quay and evading all efforts to drive them up a ship's gangway. When the foreman stevedore arrived, he knew what to do. He picked up the ram and carried it up the gangway, and the flock followed close on his heels.

Passing through Gravesend in the nineteen-thirties, we saw the launches of the Port Health Authority. Administered by the City of London Corporation, this organization keeps an omniscient eye on imported foodstuffs and other matters affecting London's health, but as far as ships are concerned its activities are centred in a hulk lying off Gravesend. In 1969 this hulk, *Hygiea*, was abandoned and Port Health launches operate from a shore base.

If a ship's complement is more than a hundred she will probably carry a doctor, and he is the liaison officer with the Port Health Authority. In smaller vessels the master assumes such duties. A certificate that the ship is free from infectious diseases saves the delay of a medical examination by the Port Health doctor of each person on board. A ship with a clean bill of health enters the port flying the yellow flag "Q" of the International Code, which means "My ship is healthy and I require free pratique." On seeing this, the Port Authority's launch puts off with the visiting doctor.

Before the war a river postman, the last of five generations of his family so employed, used to row daily from London Bridge to Limehouse and back again delivering letters to ships in the Pool. Today, letters are usually sent to ships via their London agents.

In the bad old days of chronic unemployment, watermen would sometimes scull slowly along the tideline seeking bluey, valuable copper and brass scrap. Luters were employed to sweep concrete barge hards at low water, clearing away the mud with enormous squeegees.

Another group of individualists in pre-war days (and probably still today) were the piermasters in charge of the floating piers. Dealing at one moment with fare-paying old ladies and with tough tugmen the next, they had to be very flexible. I once had an encounter with one rather abrasive character who used to boast of his tact. As official host to a party of important visitors touring the Port, I delayed their landing at his pier, which was crowded with noisy children just disembarked from a public launch. And I asked the piermaster to clear the pier as tactfully as possible so that I could land my party with decorum. "Leave it to me, sir", he replied. He took a deep breath and let fly: "Now, if you little bastards aren't off this pier in one blee'n minute, God alone knows what I won't do to you." Within seconds he came back to me. "All gone, sir", he said, with the satisfaction of a job well done. In fairness, I must add that he was not typical of river piermasters.

A sideline of watermanship is swan upping. These birds are owned either by the Crown or the Dyers' and Vintners' Companies. In July, watermen, in traditional garb and flying significant pennants, capture and mark cygnets. Among their memories was the pair of

A new PLA craft, designed and equipped to collect driftwood and floating rubbish from the tidal Thames, undergoing trials in Tilbury docks.
Photo: Port of London Authority

swans which regarded themselves as river craft and took it as a matter of course that the dockmaster would lock them with barges into the Surrey Docks.

The Doggett's Coat and Badge Race, run annually by Thames watermen not more than a year out of their time, ie their apprenticeship, demands not only sculling prowess but also a knowledge of the strength and set of tidal currents. It is rowed under the auspices of the Fishmongers' Company from London Bridge to Chelsea. The race was founded by Thomas Doggett, a much acclaimed eighteenth-century actor, to commemorate the accession of George I. The prize consists of a red coat with a large silver arm badge. A list of the winners has been kept since 1791.

The post-war wind of change has blown as strongly through forecastles of the seven seas as across the continents. Before the war, foreign seamen were indeed the simple sailors of tradition. Prominent among such men were the Lascars. In some of the old-established companies, whole families from grandfather down to grandsons might be carried in the same ship. Their loyalties were demonstrated by the Lascar deck hand who, when asked his nationality, replied "Me P&O, sahib." I used to shiver in sympathy to see them walking round the Tilbury or Royal Docks quays with their flimsy cotton draperies flapping in a strong east wind. Lascar crews held an annual parade at the docks to commemorate the martyrdom of Hassan and Hussein, grandsons of Mohammed, in the seventh century. The stewards in many of the east-bound ships were Goanese, gentle little men, Roman Catholics to a man.

Some ships in the Far East trade employed Chinese seamen. As far back as the eighteenth century the Honourable East India Company made use of them at a time when Canton was the only Chinese port open to foreigners. Sometimes these ships had their European crews savagely reduced by the press gangs of the East Indies squadron of the Navy, and Lascars or Chinese had to be recruited. The Company disclaimed liability for them when the ships paid off until 1814, when Wilberforce and public opinion succeeded in getting an Act passed whereby the Company had to be responsible for their welfare while awaiting a passage home. Before the war, Chinese seamen used to put little offerings of food in the engine rooms to placate the devils inside the engines.

Gone are the Pierhead Jumps—pathetic figures waiting on the pierhead as the ship locked out. Short of a full crew, the master would call out: "Deckhand (or fireman) wanted." One of the group would board the vessel, usually wearing all his worldly wealth and ready to go to some unknown destination without proper kit or equipment. Modern organization has laid these pitiful spectres of the past.

Overleaf: *Swan uppers of the Vintner's and Dyers' City Companies on the Thames in 1959.* Courtesy, Museum in Docklands.

Master Mariners 9

TO THE twentieth-century ear, outraged by the discordances of a utility age, there is a faint but delightful suggestion of nursery rhyme about the grandiloquent titles of some of the livery companies, particularly those whose members deal in the less-dignified articles of trade. They seem to have a background of pale ghosts, like Dick Whittington, Simon Salterne or the Burgomaster of Hamelin, whose voices, whispering from the latticed windows overhanging the quaint streets of tradition, still have an occasional say in their deliberations. There is one London livery company, however, which lacks this medieval background, but to whose members the voice of far older traditions speaks clearly and authoritatively. This company is the Honourable Company of Master Mariners.

It may well be asked why master mariners, members of one of the oldest, the most important and the highest venerated profession in the long story of these islands, should have left the foundation of their company until as late as 1926. Perhaps the delay was due to the itinerant nature of their calling; perhaps it required a First World War and the threat of a second to bring home to them how important they ranked in the economy of a race that lived only by ships. The idea of a company of master mariners was first advanced in 1921, during an after-dinner speech by Sir Robert Burton Chadwick. This was followed by an article advocating the suggestion in *Lloyd's List* in 1922. After a volume of correspondence (men of action rarely write to the Press unless they are deeply stirred), an exploratory meeting was held in London the following year, with Sir Robert Burton Chadwick in the chair. As a direct outcome of this meeting, The Company of Master Mariners was registered in 1926; and so the first London livery company to be formed for some two hundred years came into being. Nomination for membership is open to any master mariner of British nationality, with certain reservations regarding certificates, but the present maximum membership is limited to six hundred. The offices of the infant company were established in Leadenhall Street, the court meeting in premises placed at their disposal by the Corporation of Lloyd's.

In 1933 the company felt that it had grown up, and that it now required a home of its own. A corollary to this feeling was that the home should be afloat. The company was already the owner of a number of nautical treasures, books, paintings, models, etc, and what more worthy setting for nautical treasures than a ship? A move was made towards acquiring one of the few remaining deep-water square-riggers, and at one time it seemed as if the famous old *Archibald Russell* might go into honourable retirement as the company's first Hall. But many obstacles intervened, and the Second World War made the plan impracticable.

After the war the project of a floating home was resurrected. The Admiralty was approached and, not without some concealed quakings at its temerity and faith in providence, the company purchased HM Sloop *Wellington*, 990 tons. Commissioned at Devonport in 1935 for service on the New Zealand station, and recommissioned in 1937 at Wellington, New Zealand, for further service on that station, the *Wellington* served throughout most of the war as an escort vessel. Apart from assistance in the evacuation of British troops from Le Havre, she took part in no spectacular engagements; her war record was one of continuous and efficient routine service, like so many of the members of the company that now owns her.

Acquiring the ship was only the first of the problems to be overcome before the company could, so to speak, put its feet on its own mantelpiece. Bare steel plates and the grim austerity of a paid-off warship were not suitable furnishings for a livery hall, and an appeal for subscriptions towards a conversion and maintenance fund was launched. Thanks to the generosity of several shipping companies and associated interests enough money was raised to put the work in hand.

On 9th December, 1948, the *Wellington* was towed up the Thames on a flood-tide of good will, fetching up in a haven of good wishes alongside the Victoria Embankment opposite Temple Station. She is the handsomest of the ships moored in King's Reach and does the Thames credit. Thanks to the courtesy of the Company I was permitted in 1950 to visit the ship. I am not quite sure what I expected; perhaps my mixed anticipations were coloured by memories of the discomfort of wartime service in a sister ship in the winter North Sea, and perhaps by more luxurious recollections of certain boisterous evenings in a floating yacht club. I certainly had no expectation of finding the quiet, exquisite and dignified beauty which is what the love and patience habitually devoted by master mariners to their charges have created in the *Wellington*'s interior.

The *Wellington* was converted in Chatham Dockyard, and with wartime remembrance of the somewhat empirical approach to refitting jobs then exhibited by some dockyard mateys, I had entertained apprehensions about the quality and nature of the conversion. But a new generation of dockyard mateys seems to have grown up, and in any case I might have known that a company that could draw upon the services of masters in the many arts and crafts ancillary to shipbuilding and ship repair would allow them to take a personal and detailed interest in the conversion of a ship which was to become symbolic of all ships.

The first thing to strike the visitor boarding the *Wellington* is the meticulous order of the ship's furnishings and exhibits and the intensive cleanliness, which seems to glow like a white flame. No mean effort this on the part of the ex-petty officer ship-keeper and his wife, then the only permanent residents.

The ship's office, superbly panelled, must be one of the most difficult places in London in which to concentrate on paper work. Rippling water reflections flit through the ports and scurry light-heartedly across the bulkheads. From outside come the occasional yelp of a tug whistle, the lap and gurgle of passing barges and the mutter of engines. The office floor occasionally hints at a move-ment, faint but unmistakable, as if the Thames is gently nudging the *Wellington* to remind her that office floors are sometimes decks and that she is still all ship.

Many of the treasures of the company were already on view when I visited the ship—the beautiful model of the famous *Torrens*, the barometer from the same ship, Sir John Lavery's fine picture showing the scene at the Mansion House in 1932 when the then Prince of Wales, the Company's first master, received the Grant of

HQS Wellington, *the floating guild hall of the Company of Master Mariners, moored in the Thames opposite the Temple.*

Livery from the Court of Aldermen of the City of London, other paintings, models, and books. The fine teak staircase, a gift from a member, came from the *Viper*, formerly employed on the Ardrossan to Belfast service. It leads from the upper to the lower decks and thence down to the lounge and the court room. Its simple beauty blends perfectly with its new home.

I have left the most difficult description to the last. When I read before my visit that the court room occupied the *Wellington*'s former engine and boiler rooms I had my doubts, for a setting designed for machinery and furnaces hardly commends itself at first thought as a suitable site for the hall of a livery company. But the design of the room was envisaged with brilliant imagination, which, while appreciating the need to preserve the ship atmosphere, understood the importance of introducing the grace and dignity of an earlier age. Panelled throughout in oak, fifty feet long and thirty feet wide, and capable of seating some 120 persons, it has a restrained beauty that inspires a lowered voice. On the front of the dais at the far end of the room is a magnificent carving of the company's arms, somewhat spoiled by a too-faithful rendering in wood of the heraldic flags. The company's early plans were to play an increasingly bigger part in the encouragement and training of sea-minded British youth, and the importance of its deliberations had in this lovely room a worthy setting.

The establishment of the Honourable Company of Master Mariners in their own headquarters ship was an important step in the campaign to improve the social and professional status of a calling which, more than any other, had to attract the right type of recruit if the British way of life was to persist. Many writers of fiction have found it difficult to create credible master mariners; against the yo-heave-ho atmosphere must be grafted something of a scientist, an astronomer, a meteorologist, a mathematician, an accountant, an electrical engineer, a commander of men and a man of wide general knowledge. For centuries master mariners dumbly felt that they were excluded, except perhaps in time of war, from that public recognition of good work which commonly fell to the lot of the landsman. The devotion and inspiration of Coombs and likeminded seamen between the world wars planted a sapling, and the *Wellington* was its fruition.

Among the many outstanding master mariners of the Thames whom it was my privilege to know and to call my friends over the years were some who particularly come to mind. There was Captain Robert Brooks, OBE, salvage expert extraordinary, and Captain G. R. Rees, Port Salvage Officer, Commander Joseph Russel Stenhouse, DSO, DSC, OBE, Croix de Guerre, Polar Medal, BD, whose colourful exploits in all corners of the globe would fill a book on their own, Captain A. G., Course, dockmaster and one of

London's most colourful characters, who like many began his seagoing career in sail, and Captain E. E. Owen, OBE, JP, who was Ruler of the Pilots from 1932 to 1954. Then there was Captain C. E. Irving, CB, RD, RNR, who after half-a-lifetime of seafaring worldwide, including serving in *Cutty Sark*, became the doyen of the Thames Pleasure Boats, Captain J. B. Frost, another outstanding seaman from the age of sail but best remembered as Dockmaster at Tilbury, Captain W. H. Coombs, CBE, one-time Secretary of the Officers' Union and founder of the Navigators' and General Insurance Company, whose contribution to the smooth running of ships worldwide was quite outstanding, and Captain C. M. Renaut, whose superbly accurate memories of the Thames in the last century pictured fine-lined ships, figureheads and tall masts with a background of a wind-web of sail.

Space will not allow me to tell the fascinating stories of even this handful of friends in full and in detail, and so I have selected a few who seem particularly interesting in the context of the Port of London.

In an age noted for its increasing ability to destroy, a wise providence has decreed that the power to restore shall lag not too far behind. It was my good fortune to know a man who had spent a lifetime in the service of order, recovery and repair. This good Thamesman, Captain Robert Brooks, OBE, retired from the Port of London many years ago. He had served the Thames as Marine Salvage Officer throughout one of the most severe and protracted tests ever inflicted on a port salvage service.

Believing that Brooks, awake or asleep, had his mind occupied with salvage problems, I can only assume that his profession had some slight affinity with hospital nursing—and, indeed, in many respects the two vocations are not dissimilar. It is a fact that he was deeply interested in salvage from the day in 1904 when he first went to sea. But there was a master mariner's certificate and other matters to be attended to first.

In 1913 he left more orthodox seafaring and joined the Liverpool Salvage Association's *Ranger* as Chief Officer. He liked the taste of his first undertaking with this ship—the successful salving of the Red Star liner *Gothland*, wrecked on the Scillies—and he never lost the flavour. After assisting to salve the Anchor liner *California* at Tory Island, Brooks assumed command of the Association's salvage vessel *Linnet*. This move coincided with developments in the First World War, and the ship and her new master were absorbed by the Royal Fleet Auxiliary Service and sent to the Dardanelles.

Captain Brooks now encountered the difficulties of marine salvage under fire; the lessons he learned were to be put to good use in later years. He salved a number of vessels, winding up his service in those deadly narrow waters by helping to lift the last of the Allied troops evacuating the peninsula. Among other jobs which followed was the salving of the *Araby*, stranded in Boulogne Harbour. He was to come to know intimately another *Araby* of the same line, also in need of his attentions. Near the end of the First World War he became salvage officer to the Admiralty, an appointment which took him to many casualties in several different waters. After the war he took a hand in tidying up the seaways, clearing Captain Fryatt's immortal *Brussels*, the equally renowned *Vindictive* and other block ships from Belgian harbours. For these services he was created an Officer of the Crown of Belgium.

We must pause here to review the work of fate in this man in the making. A master mariner with a passionate interest in salvage had been afforded every opportunity to meet and overcome the problems attendant on ship recovery and wreck clearance in peace and war. He had had no text book to assist him, for almost every wreck at sea presents hitherto unmet difficulties. Now equipped

Captain Robert Brooks, who made a valuable contribution to the war effort in salvaging many wartime wrecks in the Thames for repair and re-entry into service, and who eventually cleared the remaining wrecks in the tideway.
Courtesy: Museum in Dockland

with a vast reservoir of practical experience, he needed only local knowledge to be of full service to the Thames in the supreme test.

In 1922 Captain Brooks was appointed Assistant Mooring and Wreck Raising Officer to the Port of London, and for the next seventeen years he pitted his wits and experience against the tricks of tide, scour, fog and gale to keep open Thames ship channels. As a result, when the Second World War exploded, the most gravely threatened vital area round the coasts of the United Kingdom had a salvage officer as superbly trained for the work as if his career had been planned to that end from his first day at sea.

I have already told* in broad outline the story of the Port of London Salvage Service, and how, working in collaboration with the Admiralty Salvage Service with whom the Port of London Authority had a wartime agreement, it kept open the vital shipping channels in the face of the utmost that could be done by an unscrupulous enemy armed with bomb and mine. It was Captain Brooks who, seeing an enemy reconnaissance plane while he was salving the ss *Dagenham* in the Thames Estuary, prudently moved the wreck upstream so that the bombers which later dropped flares at the original site found no victim. On another occasion, he and his men burnt the soles of their boots in extinguishing a fire aboard a collier. It was Captain Brooks and his crew who saved some thirty-six vessels and helped another forty-six, while nearly six hundred tugs, barges and other small craft were raised from river and docks. On the lighter side, it was Brooks who incurred official wrath by what was called "the unofficial landing of foreign cattle". He had found a cow and its calf aboard a wrecked and sinking ship and had pushed them overboard to swim ashore.

The many wartime honours and awards made to members of the Thames salvage service were virtually earned by Brooks, for he was the unchallenged leader of those gallant crews, and in experience, technical skill, fortitude, tenacity and personal courage he yielded to none who served under him. For his wartime services, Captain Brooks was made an OBE, but his work was not yet finished. For five years after the end of hostilities he moved through the graveyard of ships in the Estuary raising or dispersing casualties still endangering shipping using the channels.

Another master mariner who was also a salvage expert successfully carried out one of the most difficult recovery operations ever undertaken in the Thames. He was Captain G. R. Rees, who eventually became Director of Marine Services.

During the war, in an attempt to defeat aerial minelayers, a number of forts had been built, floated out to strategic sites in the estuary and sunk. When the war ended, they were disarmed and

The Thames on Fire by L. M. Bates (Terence Dalton Ltd, 1985).

left in situ. In those days, before the port limits were extended, only one, the Great Nore Towers, came within the province of the Port of London Authority. Trinity House took the opportunity to light the tower as a beacon warning against the Nore Sand, replacing the old Nore Light vessel, withdrawn in 1943. The fort, with the profile of a science-fiction giant spider, consisted of seven towers, each formed of four heavily reinforced concrete legs supporting gun platforms, crew quarters, etc, connected by flying bridges. (See page 38.)

In 1953, the mv *Baalbek*, groping her way out of the fog-bound river, collided with one of the towers, causing it and another to collapse with the tragic loss of four of the fort's watchkeepers. The PLA at once asked the Government to remove the wreckage and what was left of the fort as a menace to navigation. On the principle that what the eye does not see, the heart does not grieve over, the Government merely cut off the tower legs and removed the superstructure. On the river bed remained seven hollow cruciform reinforced concrete bases composed of four arms, each approximately 82 feet long, 7 feet wide and 7 feet deep. Each base weighed about 175 tonnes when sunk and had later been surrounded and covered by more than 1,000 tonnes of rubble.

For the port this was no solution since the bases would prevent dredging to maintain the statutory depth at that point. Accordingly, in 1959, do it yourself was decided on. Captain G. R. Rees, the Port Salvage Officer, began the task of lifting the obstructions. Divers reported that some of the bases had been fractured by the explosive charges used to cut the legs, allowing sand and mud to accumulate inside up to a weight of over 400 tonnes. Also, some of the arms were broken, but still joined by the reinforcements.

The Authority's powerful salvage vessel *Yantlet* and a fleet of salvage lighters were assembled. But work had to be intermittent because of the need for calm weather and suitable tides. It eventually took three summers to complete the job. On one occasion the *Yantlet* and two lighters, aided by the rising tide, were slowly lifting a base out of its bed of rubble—the foredecks of the lighters awash and daylight showing under their sterns—when one of the lifting lugs on the base pulled out. The *Yantlet's* bows shot out of the water and the two lighters suddenly took the full load and became almost vertical. Then their lugs broke off and they, too, tried to take off. Another time, five lighters dealing with one of the bases all had their bows under water; in one, it was almost lapping into the accommodation hatchway. Two of the older lighters, their hulls weakened by years of punishing work, wept copiously at the strain and only constant pumping kept them afloat.

But in Captain Rees the same spirit which inspires Welsh rugby football teams was strong, and he never even contemplated

defeat. Despite many misadventures, the work was finished in the summer of 1961. I watched the last base, slung beneath a staggering scrum of salvage craft, pass upstream to be beached amidst the triumphant yowling of steam whistles.

The divers had had the worst job, and Captain Rees told me he always knew how things were going in the depths by what came up to him over the intercom. If all was going according to plan, there would probably be snatches of a hummed refrain; if the reverse, the language was usually unprintable. One of the divers preparing for a long stay brought what he thought were his own provisions, only to find that he had instead a plentiful supply of cat food.

The Thames produced its usual little surprise at the end. Inside the last bit of loose wreckage, a steel catwalk, to be brought up were found a six-foot conger eel and a two-foot ragworm!

In the early nineteen-fifties I found the focal point of much nautical skill, much marine coming and going, in the office of the Ruler of Pilots on the west side of the Royal Terrace Pier at Gravesend. I knew of no more pleasant place to attract the ship-lover. Across the river was the Tilbury Landing Stage, where the pageant of ocean travel began and ended on nearly every tide. Past the windows in those days streamed the world's finest panorama of shipping to the accompaniment of the fascinating background noises of sirens, throbbing engines and creaking sprits from a few sailing barges then still in commission. On the office walls were some fine old prints and historic charts.

The Ruler of Pilots responsible for the administration of the London Pilotage Service was then the late Captain L. E. Owen, OBE, JP. He had served his time as an apprentice in the three-masted barque *Ashmore* in the hard days of colonial trading under sail, and his life in the half-deck conformed to the pattern of so many other square-riggers—virtually no pay, poor conditions and, above all, poor food.

Much has been written about the value of training in sail, but those who advocate it as a sound basis for modern seamanship seem, to my mind, to lose sight of the fact that character, determination and other virtues usually accorded the sail-trained seaman were engendered not so much by the type of vessel in which he served as by the conditions that ensured the early elimination of the weak. Captain Owen later served as first and second mate in some of the famous "Lochs" in the Australian wool trade before going into steam. He entered the London Pilotage Service in 1908 and after becoming choice pilot to the Royal Mail Steam Packet Company and other lines, he was appointed Ruler of Pilots in 1934, retiring in 1952. He was much sought after as an after-dinner speaker, and his salty wit was quoted up and down the tideway.

Like all master mariners, Captain Owen had had adventures and he ran true to type in keeping them to himself. I did, however, persuade him to tell me of the occasion when, as a young pilot, he was taking a French barque out of the Thames. Neither the master nor the crew spoke a word of English, but Captain Owen found that no drawback to navigating the ship, for the *lingua franca* of the sea, made up of signs and universal sea terms, transcends the limitations of shore-based tongues.

After letting go the tow rope off Beachy Head, the ship was unable to close the tug for him to disembark because the sea was running too high. Two attempts were made to put him on board the craft with a bowline from the main yard arm, but each attempt merely resulted in a ducking. Knowing that the alternative to being taken off was an enforced passage to Australia, and in a ship in which no one else spoke English, Captain Owen decided on a drastic method of departure. He stripped and sent his clothes over to the tug in a sack and then dived over the side to be picked up by the waiting craft.

No student of nautical history will deny that seamen are usually men of vision with high standards of service; many notable sailors, in maintaining those standards, have directly benefited the nation. But back in the nineteen-fifties I met a seaman, with an office little more than a stone's throw from the river, who was unique. He had begun work which was affecting the welfare of Merchant Navy officers and, through them, the Merchant Navy itself. This man, Captain W. H. Coombs, CBE, almost single-handed had succeeded within a mere thirty years in eradicating the Merchant Navy officer's sense of neglect; in giving him the status which his sacrifices in peace and war had made long overdue.

When he left the cadet ship *Conway* in 1909, he went straight into the Hooghly Surveying Service. The ever-changing channels of one of the world's most difficult rivers were fine training for a fledgling seaman. Four years later he took this experience to sea as a junior officer in the British India Line.

Like a number of great men, Coombs was not blessed with over-many inches and his short stature delayed his dogged efforts to join the Royal Navy when the First World War broke out. But in 1916, he was commissioned and appointed to HMS *Hearty*. When the war ended, he returned to the Merchant Navy and obtained his Master Mariner's certificate.

Now comes the incident which was to change his life. He had taken up an appointment in the Chinese Customs Service and one evening was entertaining a former shipmate who had sought rather unusual relaxation in the study of life insurance. For some time, host and guest talked about mortality tables, expectations of life and other aspects of insurance—all Greek to Coombs. They next turned to the subject of a mutual acquaintance, a ship's officer who, having lost his certificate as the result of a nautical mishap, had now gone to sea before the mast—a ruined man.

"Why didn't he insure his certificate?" asked Coombs.

"No underwriter would look at such a risk", his visitor replied authoritatively.

The next morning, Coombs resigned his post, its pension rights and its security, and, hardly knowing the difference between a premium and a policy, returned to London in 1921 to launch the Navigators' and General Insurance Company, with the main object of insuring the certificates of Merchant Navy officers against suspension or cancellation. The scheme was a success right from the start. Then policy holders began to refer to themselves as members of the company and sought advice on income tax, workmen's compensation and other shore-conceived problems. Legal cases began to come the way of the company, and Coombs was appalled at some of the revelations about officers' treatment and conditions. He decided to do two things. The first was to write *The Nation's Keymen* (in ten days), and nine thousand copies went out. Then he read for the Bar, the better to equip himself for what he had begun to see was to be his life mission. He was called to the Bar in 1933.

Before then, in 1928, he had helped to incorporate the Officers' Federation, which included the Navigators' and General. The first fruit of this Federation was a petition delivered to Parliament in 1933. For the first time in centuries, the petition was delivered by water. The Press flocked to publicize the tug chartered for the occasion. In due course, the Officers' Federation was granted its right place on the Maritime Board, and the officers' case was pushed with unflagging persistence. Eventually, pensions, security and most of the benefits demanded by Coombs in his book became realities. And with this conclusion to a long and gallant fight came the Second World War.

Captain Coombs was now something of an international figure and was in great demand by committees and conferences. Aerial attack completely destroyed the headquarters of the Navigators', but kind friends at Lloyd's and elsewhere enabled the company to carry on. As a now trusted and well-known leader, he broadcast to the masters of ships whose countries had been over-run, appealing to them to bring their vessels to Britain. He made similar broadcast appeals from New York.

In 1942, he felt that the time had come to please himself, and he sailed as staff captain in the Blue Funnel liner *Priam*. The voyage had its moments, for the weather caused a cargo of tanks in the 'tween decks to break adrift and some of them finished up on top of a consignment of land mines and detonators, where they rattled about for the next few days until the ship made port. In 1943, he resigned the secretaryship of the officers' union, receiving the honour of becoming President, and then he was off to sea again. His final sea service was as staff commander of a landing ship in the Normandy invasion.

After the war, he continued to work for the interests of Merchant Navy officers. He had helped to bring together the founder members of the Honourable Company of Master Mariners, on the court of which he served for over twenty years. Recognition of what this island people owed him came in 1948 when he was made a CBE.

The sea is still the main pathway along which the world's trade travels, and Captain Coombs did much to ensure that ships and their complements are able to operate safely and smoothly.

Personalities 10

THE previous chapter about my friends, all master mariners of London River, must not give the impression that these men were the only outstanding personalities among the people of the river. There were others who went to sea in a different capacity, notable watermen whose stories marched with the tides, and longshoremen who nevertheless influenced much that went on afloat. Many distinguished and gallant senior naval officers have been intimately connected with the tideway. Yet, among the rivermen who manned the Port of London during the war, one spoke of "The Admiral". And they spoke with affection. He was Admiral Sir Martin E. Dunbar-Nasmith, VC, KCB, Flag Officer in charge of the London Naval Command from the summer of 1941 to the end of the war.

His was no easy task, for he had one of the most complex commands falling to the lot of a naval officer*. The purely naval organization alone under his orders consisted of a surprising number of diverse units. There were paymasters and victualling staff to attend to the needs of warships putting into London for repair or overhaul; naval and civilian staff co-ordinating ship repairs and shipbuilding; a large minesweeping flotilla which daily swept the tidal Thames, and auxiliary mine-watching and bomb disposal officers; degaussing ranges; large training establishments; stores and ammunition depots; naval balloon stations; a large convoy-routing organization; the Thames Naval Patrol Service; signals staff; quarters for seamen and Wrens; and, nearer D-Day, the immense and complicated loading, embarkation and marshalling programme of the armada that sailed from London.

The commercial business of the Port of London was carried on during the war by the Port Emergency Committee, which consisted largely of members of the Port of London Authority. With them the admiral maintained the closest co-operation. Most of the many ship-repair and shipbuilding firms along the Thames worked during the war entirely on Government vessels and therefore mainly came under his orders. During the early days of his command the measures taken to defend the Port against possible invasion demanded his co-operation with the military services, and the 24th Battalion, City of London, Home Guard, was recruited with the specific intention of being placed under the admiral's com-

*The Thames on Fire by L. M. Bates (Terence Dalton Ltd, 1985).

Admiral Sir Martin Dunbar-Nasmith (left) *and Admiral E. C. Boyle, in successive Naval Command of the Port during the war, presenting a commemorative plaque to Sir John Anderson and Sir Douglas Ritchie of the PLA.*
Courtesy: Museum in Dockland

mand if the threatened invasion took place. Pilots, dockmasters, towage and lighterage contractors, in fact, most of the men and undertakings making up the Port of London, owed him some measure of allegiance.

This complicated pattern of sailors and soldiers, volunteers and civilians, men and women, was welded into a superb machine largely by the firmness, tact and efficiency of "The Admiral". We who worked closely with him remember the pride with which the 24th Battalion, Home Guard, put up the distinguishing divisional badges consisting of a fouled anchor, and the even greater pride with which the PLA Sector received a warm tribute from the admiral when they were finally stood down. We remember the quiet courtesy with which high and low were treated and how much the ex-fishing skippers, when their minesweeping trawlers had completed refitting and were ready for sea again, appreciated being invited into the admiral's private office to be asked if they were satisfied with the work done to their ships. We remember the ever-ready smile, particularly when the bombs were nearest, and his speedy arrival on the scene of any incident involving naval personnel in the London Naval Command.

The Port of London knows all these stories and still tells them. However, it was his adventures during the First World War that earned him the Victoria Cross; and his title of affection, "The Admiral", was a distinction achieved by no other naval officer.

My good friend Frank Taylor nearly lost the privilege of becoming a well-known and respected Thamesman when he ran away from a famous public school at the age of fifteen. Born beside the tideway, he wandered abroad for thirty years before he was drawn back, as all Thamesmen are finally drawn back, to the river which inspires both wanderlust and homesickness.

Frank Taylor was inclined to blame adventure books for his youthful escapades, but he admitted that the example of a schoolmate who had decamped a year earlier had something to do with it. At any rate, in 1901 he found himself employed by a farmer in New Zealand at the even then not princely wage of five shillings a week. After nine months the little restless devils began again to work in his blood and he shipped as pantry boy in a cattle vessel for South Africa. Kipling might have had this ship in mind when he wrote *Mulholland's Contract*, for the cattlemen on board showed mercy neither to the cattle nor to each other; knife, boot and fist were freely used to coerce their charges and to settle their incessant squabbles. Young Taylor had seen enough of cattleship life by the time the vessel reached the Cape and he quitted her and made his way up country to Zululand soon after the end of the South African War.

This bloodstained territory was only then beginning to come under white man's law, and in some of the more remote parts orders were still liable to be enforced by the bullet or the assegai. Frank Taylor divided his time between looking after a trading store and herding cattle. While on a hunting trip he experienced one of the first of many coincidences. On the lonely veldt he came across a rough pioneer memorial to the schoolmate who had left a year before he, and who had been killed in an affray with the Zulus.

Frank Taylor liked the free life and might have settled down to serious cattle ranching had it not been for the appearance of the cattle tick among the Zululand herds. Alarmed by the rapid increase of the pest, the farmers commissioned young Taylor to try to confine its ravages by fencing in an appreciable piece of Africa. With metal stanchions, barbed wire and the help of an army of Africans he completed the task in good time, only to find that the pest had already broken out in herds outside the enclosure. Disgusted with the African pattern, he returned by a devious route to New Zealand. There he entered the dairy trade. His wild oats seemed to have withered in the heat of the veldt, for he worked to such good effect that in 1930 he was appointed Inspector of Dairy Produce in the Port of London for the New Zealand Government, and so returned at last to his native Thames.

For 20 years Frank Taylor worked in London's dairy produce world, of which the Thames and Tooley Street were the main thoroughfares, and he was known and his opinions respected wherever Londoners met to discuss New Zealand butter and cheese. He was known, however, to a much wider circle as an enthusiastic collector of Thamesiana—books, pictures, legends, customs and men. On this ebb tide you might find him shooting downstream with his good friends, the Thames police; on that flood he would be photographing some tugmaster as he persuaded the Thames to give his unwieldy tow a last shove into some difficult berth; and I know that at least one week-end found him being fearfully seasick in a spritsail barge on passage from London to Colchester. His seekings and findings were largely recorded by his camera and he had some nine hundred slides with which he lectured about his hobby. And let me admit without shame that we other men of the Thames, some of us with nearly a lifetime's experience of the river, could usually learn something from Frank Taylor's lectures, for although he returned to the tides fairly late in life he had wooed them unremittingly.

It was during his early reconciliation with the Thames that he encountered another coincidence. On a camping holiday in the upper reaches he sought shelter from an approaching storm in a lock keeper's cottage. In the course of conversation he discovered that the lock keeper, now living in almost idyllic peace, had been one of his shipmates in the roaring, brutal cattle ship.

In 1948 Frank Taylor temporarily returned to New Zealand, travelling via Canada and the United States on a six months' lecture tour. Facilities offered by the Port of London, where so much of the New Zealand dairy trade is handled, featured prominently in his talks. But he took care to cater for the average New Zealander's love for and interest in the motherland by including in his lectures much of the tradition and rich history of the Thames. The cynics who claim that there is no sentiment in business are almost daily contradicted by the trade between New Zealand and the United Kingdom, and Frank Taylor's audiences were as interested in past pageantry as in modern refrigeration.

In New Plymouth, NZ, coincidence appeared again. Among his slides was one showing Lady Hoby's tomb in Bisham Abbey; the lady is associated with a grisly story of nocturnal Thames-side apparitions. After his lecture a member of the audience approached him and claimed the unhappy lady as one of his ancestors. The churchyard of St Mary's at Karori, a suburb of Wellington, provided Frank Taylor with another Port of London link. There he saw a memorial erected by a grief-stricken husband and father to commemorate the loss of his wife and three children in the *London* in 1866. Built by Money Wigram at Blackwall to pioneer a new line of steamers to Australia by way of the Cape, she was lost in the Bay of Biscay; sixteen sailors and three passengers alone survived out of her complement of 258.

Back in this country after his tour, Frank Taylor found the Thames more than ever to his liking. And he began to ask himself why he need leave it at the end of each day. Unlike many of us who are content to let our dreams remain idle, he took action, and while you and I were either paying fancy prices for accommodation in London or enduring wearisome journeys to and from the suburbs, he was snug in a charming flat on the roof of a Thames-side warehouse. His guests were numerous, for he was gregarious, as are all true Thames-siders; the visitors ranked high and low, for he returned the New Zealander's gift of being able to mix his company without ill effects. His flat was approached by a cheerless flight of stone warehouse steps which gave his guests no indication of what awaited them at the top. There they found a veritable Thames treasure house containing worth-while pictures, lovely old glass, Dresden china, a collection of beautiful period fans, and about eight thousand books. The overflow from his bookcases was housed in his den in what he called his "butter box library", and I can recommend both the convenience and appearance of a neat range of commercial cartons filled with books.

In another room he developed and enlarged his photographs to add to his ever-growing collection of slides. Posterity will learn a lot about the Thames through the medium of his diaries, in which he faithfully recorded details of each day's events since 1939; no other person has read them, and on his death they were to be sealed for a hundred years.

Soon after he had retired, a domestic tragedy called him back to New Zealand, and he never returned. But we old river hands remember his intense love for the old river.

In my writing about the Thames I have frequently mentioned the Lookout at Gravesend waterfront—the venerable annexe to the Clarendon Hotel fitted out like a ship, where the world's largest collection of merchant vessel figureheads and many other nautical treasures were once displayed. Since I first visited the Lookout some years before the war, it had become famous, and pictures of its figureheads have smiled, frowned or pouted from the pages of not only the popular press but also of more discerning journals at home and abroad. They were featured by film and television companies and several were on show at the Festival of Britain Exhibition. When the Lookout was closed in 1959, the figureheads migrated to the *Cutty Sark* at Greenwich.

Captain Long John Silver, the owner of the collection, had become equally famous. But it is regrettable that his fame was engendered merely by his collection. Casual visitors to the Lookout were prone to look somewhat sideways at him, simply because they could not understand him; few of them realized that he was the brightest jewel among the exhibits. Journalists sometimes drew upon their imagination for his background, not infrequently describing him as a retired mariner, taking care to mention the black patch over his left eye and his skull-and-crossed-bones tiepin. Perhaps they could be forgiven, for a dwelling containing a fully equipped ship's bridge and hundreds of priceless nautical relics appeared to be better copy than the owner.

It is no easy matter to sketch the character of this once well-known Thames-side personality. If you were not interested in ships or the collector's world, and preferred to discuss politics or the international situation, he was not for you. Even some of his friends who thought they knew him well sometimes asked themselves what really lay behind this mixture of shrewdness and exhibitionism. Some sought motives for his unorthodox approach to life. Why, they asked, was he a week-end roaring, ranting Thames-sider when, during the week, he was a typical City business man? Mystified, they asked why he had adopted the *nom de mer* (as he called it) of Long John Silver. He was not very forthcoming about his past, but, bit by bit, I got the story out of him.

In the old days of peace and prosperity Captain John, when ten years of age, lost his left eye through an accident with a toy gun. Some divinity, as is often the case whatever Hamlet may have said, was merely doing the rough hewing, for from this cause Captain John effected the shaping of his own ends in later years. Any stolid boy would have been sadly affected by such a loss; the shock to a highly sensitive youngster was all the greater. Team games for him ceased to exist, and even ordinary boyish companionships were largely denied him through the inherent callousness of the young male. As a result, he became self sufficient, being driven more into himself as the full extent of his disability came home to him.

The boy had always had a passionate interest in ships and indeed, up to the time of the accident, had been determined to make the sea his career. As some solace for his affliction, a doting and well-to-do father bought him a magnificent scale-model steamship worthy of gracing any Cockspur Street window. Thus we have an imaginative boy, debarred from normal boyish pursuits and companionship, and interested in the sea, given a collector's piece. But more than that went to the moulding of Captain Long John Silver.

Soon after the accident, the family migrated to Westbrook and the lonely little lad found an absorbing hobby in the stream of shipping entering and leaving the Thames Estuary. Most of his spare time was spent on the North Foreland with the telescope which ranked only second to the model ship; he began to spot and study house flags and ship silhouettes, and to read the shipping papers, until he could beat the coastguards at their own game.

Some of the marine collection formerly in the Lookout, Gravesend. The figureheads went to the Cutty Sark, the rest to the National Maritime Museum.

It was not long before the master of his preparatory school discovered his hobby and, unconsciously anticipating the Ship Adoption Society by many years, based his geography lessons on the passing ships, an informal class being held twice a week on the North Foreland; and firing master and pupils with his enthusiasm and his expert knowledge was the quiet, nervous boy with the large telescope. Not a little of his sense of inferiority was shredded and blown out to sea by the confidence which these moments of leadership inspired in him. As some small proof of his changing

109

outlook, we have the testimony of his sister in the matter of a certain undergarment she was making in the fine white material that ladies then used for certain undergarments. Leaving it unguarded on her worktable for a while, she returned to find a large triangle, suitable, say, for the jib of a model yacht, cut from the middle of it.

His proposed sea career abandoned, the embryo individualist completed his education in London and entered the family business. He was still a somewhat nervous and retiring young man, acutely conscious of the glass eye that only partly disguised his loss and was a source of continual discomfort. Perhaps it was due to his friends' custom of calling him after R.L.S.'s famous character; it might have been due to contact with and reading so much about that great school for individualists—the sea; whatever the motive, he one day abandoned his artificial eye and boldly proclaimed his infirmity by wearing a black patch. Any modern psychologist would have charged him a large sum for advising this best possible treatment for his nervousness. For with the adoption of the patch, the tender plant of individualism struggling through the clay of convention came to full growth.

Not a few of the stories about Long John Silver have become legendary along Thames-side. Those who knew him became used to hearing the opening bars of *Fifteen men on a dead man's chest* as his signature tune when he used the telephone. And more than once he entertained distinguished national figures to a shrimp tea served by a Thames bawleyman clad in fisherman's garb. But the story I like best concerns the fishing net. At his former beautiful home in London near Kensington Gardens, bombed during the war and later exchanged for a flat, he had a wonderful aquarium. Returning from a business meeting in the formal clothes which were then de rigueur on such occasions, he bought a long-handled net to aid him in this hobby. Before he reached home, however, he met a band of urchins armed with jam jars and home-made nets.

"Going fishing, Guv'nor?" they chorused.

"Yus." replied John, courteously suiting his accent to his company. "Let's go to the Rahnd Pond." And for about an hour, a pleasant sight in his formal City clothes, he helped the boys to capture a number of unfortunate sticklebacks before he continued his journey home.

One year when he and his charming mate were holidaying in the Scillies, he discovered that the famous old island gigs were falling into disuse under the challenge of modern powered craft and that the equally famous old rowing races had been abandoned. He promptly offered a trophy, a large silver cup, in an attempt to revive interest in these craft. So far, so good, for this was merely a beneficent interest that any well-to-do visitor might have shown in island seamanship. But only he would have thought of calling it The Treasure Island Trophy and of filling it with imitation jewellery, beneath which were concealed seven piratical-looking bags of silver for the winning crew.

Unfortunately, space does not permit the telling of the many other stories about this prince of individualists, but he was long remembered in Morocco and other parts of North Africa for the highly unconventional and colourful atmosphere which surrounded him when he visited some of the Kaids and other notabilities there. I should like space, too, to tell the story of the findings of the Golden Cherubs, which he claimed to be the world's oldest existing merchant-ship figurehead and believed to be the work of Grinling Gibbons, and the yarns behind many other items in his collection. Many of the stories showed that behind the flippancy and exhibitionism was a good business brain, for he had never been known to pay through the nose for any marine curio he might covet. Visitors found him exceedingly generous; the clang of his bridge telegraph would bring up a steward with unlimited drink and refreshment, but he got much fun in running his hobby as cheaply as possible.

During the week, John was all convention; he lived in a conventional flat, dressed and spoke conventionally. But at weekends, down at the Lookout, he kept open house for almost anyone connected with the sea, wore a yachting cap, ranted and roared like any old shellback, flew unorthodox and sometimes outspoken flag signals from his halliards on the river bank and dispensed much rum punch.

He used to thrust his telescope at the tidal procession of ships and craft then passing his window and was invariably correct in the matters of flags, lines, tonnages, destinations and cargoes. More than once I heard him put a professional shipping man right on questions of nautical history. He usually looked considerably younger than his age, but when he was talking ships he looked as bright and youthful as a boy. It was a loss to the tideway when he died, a worthy if eccentric Thames man, in 1959.

The ever faster rate of material progress constitutes a threat to the continuity of mental development. In older and more leisurely times the reminiscences of the sage were listened to with respect, and each generation benefited to some extent from the experiences of the elders. Today the voice of the sage is drowned in the thunder of events, and with more and more effort each generation has to rediscover for itself the basic way of living. It is only in times of crises that the voice of experience commands respect.

This preamble was not inspired by any suggestion that Charles Etheredge, MBE, should have been likened to a sage—he was too

111

human and had too great a sense of humour to warrant such a description. But he was a Thamesman of long standing who had seen the change from stable conditions, hardly varied in principle for centuries, to the chromiumed haste and fluid events of the world today, and he had, perhaps, a better perspective of our progress than the members of younger generations.

All Etheredges were born with tide water in their veins. One of them was practising as a ship smith and pump maker at the beginning of the last century. That old Etheredge left his mark on the tideway, for he invented and manufactured a brail winch for spritsail barges which, in principle, was in use in the last barges. The next Etheredge was apprenticed to the old man as a pump maker, but he was too much interested in the crowded colourful life afloat in the Thames to be content to remain in a workshop and he at last wore down the opposition to his becoming an apprenticed waterman. Many tides later he came ashore to help develop the family business into a towage and lighterage, barge building and repair firm.

That brings us to the Etheredge of my time. Like his father he became an apprenticed waterman as a preliminary to joining the company, and his indentures were signed in 1896. As a boy he already had an intimate acquaintance with the tideway and remembered the old wooden paddle tugs with woodbine funnels and how they had to be pumped out every few hours. He remembered, too, the swim-headed spritsail barges and other types of craft long since vanished from the Thames scene.

Serving his time in his father's tugs he sometimes went seeking, ie hunting the tow rope of an expected inward-bound sailing vessel, and he not infrequently spent as long as three weeks in acute discomfort rolling about the Channel somewhere off the Isle of Wight. He remembered Thames watermen in the same vicinity engaged in "goozing", Thamesese for incredible voyages in skiffs to be first alongside an inbound ship to buy her surplus fat and unwanted rope. Superimposed on Etheredge's lively memories of modern warfare was his recollection of taking down to the Royal Albert Dock a number of horse boxes originally used in the Crimean War and hurriedly disinterred from Government arsenals for the use of cavalry going to the South African War.

It is, however, in the matter of marine salvage that he cherished the most entertaining memories. Despite our nostalgic glances backward at the good old days, there is no doubt that the vessels of a century ago were much more vulnerable to the perils of the sea than are ships today. The news of a hovel, as ships in distress were called by longshoremen, would excite the cupidity of all tugmen, and the prospect of a large salvage award would inspire them to resort to the most extraordinary tricks to throw possible rivals off the scent. A funnel, for instance, might be lowered and covered with canvas to give the tug, at least from a distance, the silhouette of a barge. Lights at night might be dowsed or reversed. Anchors might even be got up by hand, the cables being handled like glass to make heaving-up a noiseless operation*.

The name hovel is believed to derive from the dwellings of the old-time Deal longshoremen, famed for their highly-skilled, if sometimes piratical, salvage services to ships in trouble on the Goodwin Sands. Etheredge still chuckled at the memory of Deal hovellers, wakened in the night with news of a wreck, tearing through the streets with most of their clothing under their arms down to the beach where, up to their necks in water, their womenfolk were already launching the boats.

The older Thames watermen were often illiterate, but Etheredge maintained that their knowledge of the river was second to none. Tide-tables, for instance, rarely came within the waterman's purview, but he knew to the minute when it was time to get under way by the relationship between the level of the water and some local mark, perhaps the mooring rings on Tower Bridge.

In due course Etheredge came ashore and eventually took over the family business, by then greatly extended. It was during the First World War that he established a reputation with the Admiralty which resulted in a profitable connection for the firm. A fleet of forty-two big Rhine barges were in Rotterdam awaiting towage to this country. The craft were suitable for use only in inland waterways and tended to break their backs in a seaway. Moreover, the North Sea was then as infested with mines and submarines as it was during the Second World War. Faced with these difficulties, a number of towage firms turned down the proffered contract. With long experience of barges of all shapes and sizes, afloat and ashore, right-side up or capsized, Etheredge took on the job. He collected a crew of the toughest watermen he could find and sent them off in one of his tugs. It was typical of the master that when he found that he could not keep up with the convoy he chanced the mines and submarines and sailed independently, reaching Rotterdam safely.

The barges were specially strengthened by a means devised by Etheredge, and the first tow left for the Thames. In mid-Channel the tug crew found two destroyers sinking after fouling a minefield. Casting off the tow, the tug went in to the rescue. The skipper was peremptorily ordered to take his vessel out of danger, but being an independent Thamesman he gave serious offence to a senior naval officer by telling him to mind his own embellished business and continued with the rescue work. When all possible

*See also Chapter Fifteen.

survivors had been picked up, the tug wandered happily among the minefield until the tow was fast again. The party then continued safely to the Thames. The tug skipper received a decoration for his gallantry and an admonition for his insubordination. Forty-one barges were successfully brought over, one being sunk by a submarine. For his services in the operation, Etheredge was made MBE. As a tailpiece to the affair, he recalled that when the tug crew gathered in his office to receive their pay, they quarrelled over the shares and indulged in a right bloody free-for-all among the desks and chairs.

Since then Etheredge not infrequently acted on behalf of the Admiralty, and he and his partner rendered invaluable assistance during the last war. One imagines Whitehall viewing his entry into its offices as being like an Estuary north-easter, for he had that direct and simple approach to life and business which avoided red tape like the plague.

A backward glance through my gallery of Thames-side personalities shows that the London River boasts only swans; and, indeed, there are literally no geese in my tideway. My late good friend, Lieutenant-Commander Frank G. G. Carr, RNVR, bargeman, yachtsman, nautical author, and former director of the National Maritime Museum, must claim, for his mastery of practical and theoretical seamanship, his deep love for and understanding of small craft, his learned appreciation of the Royal and Merchant Navies' traditions, a permanent niche in this riverside record.

Carr's tutelary spirit obviously agreed with Emerson about the advantages of a wagon hitched to a star and arranged for him to have a grandfather who was an astronomer at the Royal Observatory and a mother herself born in the observatory at Cambridge; and stars, as practical aids to navigation and the subject of scholarly research, greatly influenced his life.

A rowing man of some repute at Cambridge University, Carr first made acquaintance with the delicious mystery of wind-driven craft by hoisting a mere duster of a sail in a sixteen foot skiff on the Cam during the First World War. Rigging the sail over the boom as a camp-awning, he tasted those delights of a floating home which, once enjoyed in youth, never stale. He recalled a picture of a favourite uncle angularly folded in an effort to prevent his head touching the awning, which would thereby have caused a drenching rain to percolate the canvas, and humming plaintively. "That tune sounds familiar," observed the equally uncomfortable Carr; "what is it?" The uncle grinned. "I dreamt that I dwelt in marble halls!" he replied. It was a heartening start to the gentle pleasures of boat owning.

When circumstances permit, this boat owning can be as

unremittent as malaria. Carr's next craft, acquired in 1921, was an eighteen-foot half-decker which he sailed on the Norfolk Broads. In those generous days, such a craft could be bought for £20; and in her Carr explored every corner of the Norfolk waterways. It was then that he found fresh water growing insipid, and he began to venture along the coast, getting, on one occasion, a rare fright when he was caught out between Yarmouth and Lowestoft. Carr recalled that this particular craft was an unhandy creature, but with the philosophy of the sailorman he reflected that her stubborn temperament taught him later to appreciate and enjoy sweeter and more tractable craft.

In August, 1924, he bought his first sea-going ship, the five-ton, clinker-built cutter *Lily*, born at Leigh twenty years earlier. Then knowing little of the traditions of the sea, he changed her name to *Quickstep* to commemorate another much-loved *Quickstep* which his grandfather had sailed in the Thames in the eighteen-eighties. But any shellback would have told him that bad luck invariably follows a change of name; and bad luck certainly followed in full measure.

With his father and his younger brother as crew, Carr and *Quickstep* were caught out off Orford Ness. Driving before a south-westerly gale under a tiny reefed foresail, his sea anchor long since carried away, and running off the edge of his charts, Carr hoisted a distress signal which caused a Norwegian tramp to close him. The Norwegian skipper agreeing to tow them into the lee of the land, Carr, with visions of a possible salvage claim, anxiously asked how much it would cost. "It will gost you noddings", replied the skipper. But it was to cost Carr quite a bit—and, in fact, nearly cost him his life.

The tramp, flying light and with her engines stopped, was blowing down to leeward at fearful speed, and Carr, trying to take a line, found his little craft jammed under the ship's counter where she thumped her bottom against the big propeller. All efforts to extricate *Quickstep* failed, for with the little craft sitting on her propeller the tramp was unable to manoeuvre. A rope ladder was lowered and the Norwegian implored the three to abandon ship. It was no occasion for heroics, and Carr, with the prerogative of master, sent his father and brother up the ladder to safety. Before he himself could follow, *Quickstep* suddenly broke from the embrace of the big ship, and for a few wild optimistic seconds Carr hoped that he might yet take a line and save his craft. But poor little *Quickstep* was snapped up by a North Sea wave and smashed like an eggshell on the tramp's propeller blades. Carr leaped on to the ladder as the craft plunged from beneath him, sinking instantly; the ladder, however, was foul of the rigging and in the speed of her foundering the topmast shroud caught and broke his thumb. He remembered in the hurly-burly hearing his father calling to him to abandon the yacht—"I'll buy you another boat," he yelled; "I cannot buy another son!"

When Carr came down from Cambridge in 1926 he acquired his last, and faithful, love—the ex-Bristol Channel pilot cutter *Cariad*. Like the ill-fated *Lily*, she was built in 1904. Her home port was Pin Mill on the Orwell, and she and Carr together voyaged nearly forty thousand miles round our coasts and from the Baltic to Biscay. Some of their adventures provided subjects for her skipper's subsequent writings, and details of this well-known vessel would be out of place in these notes about her owner.

Carr studied navigation and seamanship for his yachtmaster's certificate, living between August, 1926, and March, 1927, at Jack's Palace in the Commercial Road. There he learned the most important lesson of the sea—that theory can never be more than complementary to practice. So, having long cherished a distant affection for the then flourishing spritsail barge, he shipped in 1927 as mate of the *Phoenician* under the almost fabled Captain Alf Horlock.

In 1928 he made a trip as mate of the barge *Dorothea*. In the same year he received a compliment that he ranked his highest. He was then again up at Cambridge studying for his LLB Law; the printed page tasted sour after the piquant flavour of the sea, and he was spiritually at low ebb. Then, suddenly, he was electrified by a telegram from old Harry Ward (of the golden ear-rings) who watched over *Cariad* at Pin Mill. It tersely informed him that the barge *Davenport*, due to sail that night for Antwerp, was without a mate. Would he go? Carr hurled his Roman Law text book and sea boots into a bag, changed into sea-going kit and caught the last train to Ipswich. He reached the Butt and Oyster (later referred to in all good faith by a relative as The Buttoned Oyster) just before closing time. Navigating towards the bar through the fog of tobacco smoke, he found Ward, who introduced him to Tom Strange, the skipper short of a mate. He looked Carr up and down and then gave him the accolade. "Thank God!" he said in relief. "Why, I thought you were a toff. What'll you have to drink?" Carr made the trip to Antwerp with sheep dip, returning with bog ore, learning the ancient lore of the sea on deck, studying the comparatively upstart Roman Law in his watch below, and receiving wages of a pound per week.

During those happy years Carr was coming more and more to love these beautiful spritsail-rigged anachronisms. In 1929 he was seriously examining the possibilities of earning an honest living by well-planned smuggling with the aid of a Thames barge when, to his intense surprise, he learned that he had been successful in his application for the post of assistant librarian to the House of Lords. His days of sea roaming were now confined to holidays, and he settled down to write about the spritsail barge. *Sailing Barges* appeared in 1931, and something of his love for the subject, much of the essence of the craft distilled in wet and weary passages, and not a few of the grand old yarns told in the Butt and Oyster, went to its making. Brought up to date in a new edition in 1989, it still remains the standard work on these fast-dying ships*. Other books followed: *Vanishing Craft*, in 1934; *A Yachtsman's Log*, in 1935; the delightful *Yachtsman's England*, in 1936.

In May, 1947, his stars led him to his glorious haven—the post of director of the National Maritime Museum at Greenwich, beside the river at which he had so often peered from beneath the shadow of a spritsail. We of the tideway felt that the choice could not have been bettered. All who sought his help on matters nautical (and they were countless) soon realized that the museum is something more than a repository of the past. Carr interpreted his duties to include the creation of a centre of current interests of the Royal and Merchant Navies. Only thus, he maintained, could the museum preserve for posterity that commonplace of today likely to become the rarity of the future.

One of Carr's triumphs was to help the old *Cutty Sark*, fully restored and re-rigged as the supreme example of the clipper ship, to become permanently cradled in her special dock at Greenwich. He visualized her as representing the spirit of the Merchant Navy in the same way that *Victory* symbolizes the character of the Royal Navy.

When Chaucer wrote: "Therefore have I yeven thee a sufficient Astrolabie as for our orizonte compowned after the latitude of Oxenforde", he could not have foreseen modern university rivalries. But Carr, as a good Cantabrigian, might feel that he had scored over even Chaucer, for before he retired he became the virtual custodian of the Greenwich Meridian by joining the former home of the Royal Observatory with the National Maritime Museum.

His principal interest until his death was the World Ship Trust, of which he was chairman.

Although the ruffles and plumes, jaunty cloaks and jewelled swords of old were not infrequently the trappings of a timid heart, most of the sheep in former days wore distinctive sheep's clothing. It is, perhaps, a loss to the contemporary scene that we now shrink from dressing the part; knight and squire, statesman, scholar, man of action and adventure, all seek a uniform anonymity beneath the

---

*Revised edition, Terence Dalton Ltd, 1989.

sober and featureless clothes of the city. I had this thought in mind as I listened to a brief and diffident account of some of the adventures of the late Charles G. Alexander, managing director of the former fine old London towage firm of W. H. J. Alexander Ltd, owners of the famous Sun tugs. Then conforming outwardly to the pattern of thousands of other London men of business, his early life bore little resemblance to the grubbing apprenticeship to cheque book, desk and pen which was mainly their youthful lot.

Charles Alexander became an apprentice waterman and lighterman in 1900, and after storing up practical experience of the subtle business of towing he entered in due course the office of his father's firm. There he might have stayed, learning more and more about profits and expenses, and remembering less and less about the queer telepathy between a good tug skipper and his engineer, had not fortuitous circumstances called him away from his desk to fill a vacancy afloat caused by a temporary emergency in the firm's manning schedule. He liked his regained freedom of the river so much that he stayed there for the next twenty-seven years. He was acting skipper at the age of seventeen and a half years, passed for Home Trade Master and took a fair share of coasting and Continental towage work. But his richest treasury of memories centred on the Thames tideway.

It is in the stories of these men who have served the Thames so intimately that one senses the greatness of the London riverman —and particularly the continuity of his traditions. Through Alexander's yarns (and he was much more ready to talk about his former shipmates than himself) ran a thread of toughness, good sportsmanship, rough jokes, ready wit and a spirit of sturdy independence.

Charles Alexander came ashore in 1933, resigned to settling down at last to an office desk. But the Thames at war called him out again to take a command afloat in the Odyssey of the little ships. Six of the firm's tugs were asked by the Admiralty to go to the help of the beleaguered army at Dunkirk. It may be interpolated here that their combined efforts were responsible for lifting a total of 1421 men; two masters were made OBE and an engineer MBE. To return, however, to the beginning of the adventure, only five skippers were available for the six craft. At almost a minute's notice, Alexander went by car from the City office to Tilbury and, by a reshuffling of commands, was able to take over his old ship, *Sun IV*.

Sun IV was one of a big team at Dunkirk, but earlier, in 1930, Charles Alexander, then in normal command of the craft, had successfully conducted a more individual operation which still stands in the annals of the sea as a classic example of how skill, tenacity and courage can snatch victory from almost certain defeat.

At about 10.15 pm on 17th October of that year, the tugs *Sun IV* and *Sun XII*, then lying at Gravesend, learned that an oil tanker was on fire off Thames Haven. The two craft immediately got under way and found the *Elkhound*, a motor tanker with a cargo of more than 600 tons of petroleum, badly on fire in her engine-room aft, and abandoned by her crew, with the exception of the mate. Despite the imminent danger of explosion, Charles Alexander and some of his crew boarded the ship and endeavoured to extinguish the blaze. The fire, however, had taken hold of the ship's oil fuel and spread so rapidly that they were driven back.

Local authority then feared that the tanker might become a serious danger to other ships and riverside installations, and there is no doubt that, had she blown up, six hundred tons of burning spirit afloat on the tide might have presented the river with a fearful problem. It was accordingly decided to attempt to tow her out to sea. With four volunteers, the master of *Sun IV* went back on board the burning vessel, made fast the towing hawsers of the two tugs and slipped the tanker's cable. With much the same atmosphere as that surrounding a lorry transporting a ticking bomb, the tugs began to tow downstream as fast as circumstances permitted. The danger to the tugs was increased by the fact that in the more crowded reaches they had to use a short scope of rope to keep the deserted ship under control, and it was not until they reached more open water that the tow ropes could be lengthened. Although the burning ship was being towed head to wind, which helped to keep the flames from reaching the cargo, various explosions took place and flaming oil from the fuel tanks streamed down her sides.

Off the Cant Sand in the outer estuary it was decided to hold the tanker head to wind and to let her burn out. But the mate of the tanker, now a passenger on board *Sun IV*, said that the vapour-proof door of the pump room had been left open and that it was essential to close it to prevent the cargo taking fire and exploding. So *Sun IV* sent away a boat from which Charles Alexander once more boarded the burning ship and, making his way through showers of sparks from the ship's blazing woodwork, succeeded in closing and securing the vital door. A little imagination inspires the reflection that rendering a mine safe would be, by comparison, a pleasant pastime.

All night the two tugs kept the vessel head to wind, and by daylight the engine-room had nearly burned itself out. *Sun IV* went alongside and finally extinguished the remains of the fire. Both ship and cargo were undoubtedly saved in the very teeth of disaster. During the subsequent hearing of the salvage claim, the president of the Admiralty Court referred to the efficient and exceedingly gallant service of the tugmen.

The late Charles Alexander, former Managing Director of W. H. J. Alexander Ltd, who had adventures in war and peace in his Sun tugs.
Courtesy: Museum in Dockland

The salvage award to Alexander and his two crews was substantial. When counsel asked him what he would do with the money, Alexander's reply was characteristic. "Are you married?" he asked. "Yes," replied counsel. "Then", said Alexander, "don't ask bloody silly questions."

Just before the outbreak of war, I met Mr W. T. Starbuck, a Gravesender full of that old seaport's past. Back in the eighteen-eighties, he had first gone to sea in his father's collier schooners and fishing smacks, all based on Gravesend. He told me some of his father's stories about the Press Gang. Shipowners kept their apprentices out of the Navy's clutches by sleeping them at the tops of their own homes and by seeing that prime fish regularly found its way to the house of the Press Master at New Tavern Fort. Some of the stories showed the lengths to which free and easy Gravesend sailormen would go to avoid being forced into the Senior Service. On one occasion, a smack master, who was a bachelor, was about to be boarded by the Press when he casually mentioned that his wife was below, sick with smallpox. The Press hurriedly took to its oars. (Did Mark Twain hear this story from some far-roaming Gravesender and adapt it in *Huckleberry Finn*?)

Another story told of the Press searching likely hiding places in a smack by thrusting in steel-headed pikes. An apprentice hiding in a wing of the well had his arm pierced, but he valued his freedom sufficiently to endure it without uttering a sound. One of the smacks was once in collision with a collier in a dense fog off Aldeburgh Ness. The damage was severe, and the smack crew were ordered to jump for their lives to the deck of the other ship. When the roll was called, four apprentices were found to be missing. Some days later, the damaged smack arrived at Gravesend in charge of the four boys, who had improvised a collision mat from a sail. Appropriately enough, the name of the smack was *British Hero*.

The transport of cattle across the river at Gravesend by means of a crude float provided Starbuck with memories of watermen's skiffs chasing cattle swimming for freedom. He remembered the keen competition for Thames passenger traffic between the *Albert Edward* and the ill-fated *Princess Alice* in close rivalry with the *Alexandra* and the *Palmerston*. The latter two had been blockade runners freighting cotton from southern ports during the American Civil War, and had afterwards been adapted, not very successsfully, for Thames pleasure work. The *Princess Alice* provided trips to see the *Great Eastern* lying up in the Medway opposite Queenborough.

This old Gravesender spoke of the arrival of the *Thermopylae* and other famous clippers, of the departure of emigrants in auxiliary windships, of Watkins's old *Anglia* towing Cleopatra's Needle in its cylindrical vessel, of sea coal and conger eels—all waterfront topics in the old seaport last century.

Four times a day, the finger of Father Thames gently pushed round the sterns of the skiffs dotting the offshore moorings at Gravesend. And old Mr Warner used to look up from his work to watch the manoeuvre, for he had created most of those boats. Moreover, he was the last practising survivor of the boat builders who once flourished in the old port. When a child, he knew boats as other children know perambulators. His father built boats all his life, beginning with the six-strake Greenwich skiff, afterwards migrating to Gravesend to build the Gravesend waterman's skiff, a larger boat of seven strakes, 21 feet by 5 feet 6 inches by 2 feet. When I met my Mr Warner in the late nineteen-thirties, he had just retired. Sixty years earlier, he had been apprenticed to his father's business at Gravesend and, with the exception of two years' service at Tilbury during the First World War, he had built boats ever since. They were built of oak, copper fastened throughout, the timbers and knees were cut from crooks grown to the required shape and fitted to the planking by a process known as joggling. Steamed timbers never found favour with the old man.

Warner's old shop has disappeared beneath the clumsy feet of progress, but when I saw it it was said to be over four hundred years old; it was acquiring a mellowed appearance even before the Thames saw men and ships scurrying out to meet the threat of the Spanish Armada. Several times the shop escaped destruction; flaming tar barrels and fireworks threatened it on several 5th November celebrations. Warner recalled that on those occasions, a prahm might be stolen from some Norwegian ship cowering in the river, filled with inflammables and dragged blazing over the cobbles.

For over a hundred years the Warners had stood to their boats, and neither fire, flood nor hard times had driven them away from the river. But a more insidious enemy in the form of mechanization has decreed that no apprentices were there to carry on, and now few remember their name.

John Burns, in his time one of the more famous Thames-siders, died in his eighty-fifth year early in 1943. He was born in the riverside borough of Battersea and he represented Battersea in Parliament for thirty-six years. He loved and understood the Thames in all its different moods. It was John Burns who wrote: "The Thames is London and London is the Thames, and both make and are the Port of London." Much more widely quoted was his summing up of the river's role. During the First World War, he was talking to a group of oversea visitors at Westminster. A Canadian among them held forth on the majesty of the St Lawrence river, and he was followed by an American who sang the praises of the mighty Mississippi. When they had finished, John

Burns's said: "Your St Lawrence is just water. Your Mississippi is plain mud. But the Thames is liquid history."

I met John Burns only once. At a Thames-side function a grey-bearded old man in a shiny double-breasted blue suit asked me if I knew who he was. I recognized him at once and named him without hesitation. "Right", he said, without the slightest trace of gratification. Then he continued abruptly: "Have you heard the story about the Bloody Tower?" To which I replied: "Do you mean the one about the tired and dispirited Beefeater saying 'All of it, madam'?" "Yes", he said. "I made up that story. Good afternoon." And off he went. John Burns was unique.

Last in this gallery of river personalities comes my friend Jewiss, then the master of the tug *Danube III*. (I never knew his Christian name and always gave him the honorary title of captain.) One trip with him stands out in my memory. I joined his craft at Gravesend. He settled me in a corner of the wheelhouse and began to tell me of his adventures. Below the Lower Hope, a north-east gale was raising something more than a popple in Sea Reach and we prepared for trouble by letting out more towing wire. As soon as this was done, the crew of the hopper we were towing disappeared below; they knew what was coming.

Plugging seaward again, the old skipper continued his rambling tale of how he had been given a temporary RNR commission and had taken a Danube tug out to the Dardanelles during the First World War. By the time he was well into his yarn, we were climbing slowly up each oncoming wave and tobogganing down the reverse slope. Spray flicked the bridge screen like dried peas and vicious squalls shook the wheelhouse doors. But the skipper's words kept time with the reassuring beat of the engines.

When the dumping ground at D2 Buoy came in sight, he brought his well-embroidered yarn to a close with: "Then I said to my Crystal Palace gunner, 'Let him have it, boy', and his first shot hit the submarine's conning tower, and that was the last we saw of him." A long and a short blast on the steam whistle brought the hopper's crew on deck to manipulate the "doors" of their craft. They wasted no time on deck, for, washed by every wave, it was both uncomfortable and dangerous.

With the now unladen hopper high in the water and skittering about like a balloon, we turned back and, the wind now astern, found life much more comfortable. As the lights started to spring up around us in the gathering dusk, the old man eased off the wheel and chuckled. "Lemme tell you about the time . . ." he began. I have forgotten his next yarn, but I remember that he obviously enjoyed that trip almost as much as I did.

Writers and Artists   11

MANY WRITERS and artists have interpreted the strange lure of the tideway—dreamers whose skills have made visible those then unknown horizons towards which the long finger of tidal water has ceaselessly beckoned. And if the development of our sea services, and through them the export of democracy, owe anything to the writings of Kipling, Conrad, Tomlinson and a hundred others before them, then they owe nearly as much to the grandeur of Turner's river scenes and seascapes, the waterside nocturnes of Whistler, the meticulous accuracy of Wylie and many other marine artists.

A complete record of all dreamers on a Thames theme would be quite outside the scope of this work, and I must limit my writings to those authors whose work has particularly appealed to me, and those artists whom I have met. And I am not qualified to criticize such work and shall merely outline their relationship to the Thames. I begin with a successful author and former Member of Parliament who lent colour to the grey backcloth of the industrial Thames. The late Sir Alan Herbert was as well known and as much at home in the tideway as any ramping, stamping old timer of the waterfront. His biography has been written elsewhere and (I repeat) this is only a brief record of some of the occasions when he hobnobbed with Father Thames.

Sir Alan did not admit to any early urge to use the river as a medium for work and recreation. He recalled that the Round Pond was the first water to attract him; good seamanship and much luck decided the furious races in which his and his brother's toy boats were sailed. Chance first opened his eyes to the possibilities of London River. While up at Oxford, he used always to watch the Universities Boat Race from Duke's Meadows, Chiswick. After the 1914 race he walked along the Chiswick Mall with F. Anstey, the Punch writer, who told him something of riverside lore. Soon after this meeting he married, and, casting about for a suitable domicile, remembered Anstey's stories. As a result, he began married life in the first available house near Chiswick Mall.

Before he had a chance to get to know the river, he went to the Dardanelles in the First World War. It was not until he returned to London in 1918 that he began to see the river in the right perspective. He soon decided that it was wasteful not to use some of this vast expanse of water rolling past his doorstep and he bought a small seven-foot dinghy from a London store. With only book knowledge of small-boat sailing, he made a mast and sail and launched his little vessel upon what has been called the Highroad to China; steering with an oar, he made his first landfall at Westminster.

His next problem, that of many intrepid seamen faced by adverse winds and tides, was how to get back. It was solved by a kindly tug master, who, having taken the adventurer on board his craft, wrapped a large fist round the dinghy's mast and lifted the boat on to his deck, to the astonishment of Members of Parliament assembled on the Terrace. After such a voyage, Sir Alan had no chance to escape his fate and joined the ranks of those to whom small craft and the London River are irresistible.

The ownership of boats, like the possession of cars and radios, is rarely static and the Herberts soon wanted something more ambitious. The next floating acquisition was the *Ark*, a flat-bottomed canal boat with a draught of only twelve inches. She travelled many miles on the Grand Union Canal and the tideway. The epic cruise of her career was when she ventured as far as Gravesend and back.

Now a loyal and enthusiastic Thamesman, Sir Alan developed a great love for and understanding of the Thames spritsail barge. His first practical experience of these beautiful craft was as third hand (*ex officio*) in the *Paglesham* from the Surrey Docks to Colchester, with three days windbound in Sea Reach for good measure. Mr Eves, the master, had a small dog on board which Sir Alan swore could smell a buoy in the dark and which was of great help in the Swin. On other occasions, he sailed in Daniel's barges to and from Whitstable.

Encouraged by these adventures, the Herberts chartered the *Saltcote Belle*; the hold was equipped with camp beds and primus stoves, and she was their home for two glorious weeks. Herbert recalled how the skipper of this craft loved her being a "yacht" as a change from freighting cargo. The converted barge *Plinlimmon*, one-time famous Medway racer, was also chartered on several occasions. In her Sir Alan saw many of the Thames Sailing Barge Races, and he claimed to be one of the few outsiders honoured with an invitation to the Bargemen's Dinner after a race.

It was during one of these cruises in the *Plinlimmon* that disaster nearly overtook the family. With the Herberts were two children and a dachshund (the latter, presumably, to fill the role played by the dog of the *Paglesham*). During a very dirty night, with Beachy Head close under their lee, the steering chains parted and left the craft driving inshore. They were picked up with little time to spare by a boat from a collier.

Meanwhile the *Ark* had been broken up and the famous old Hammersmith firm of Cole & Son had begun to build the *Water*

Gipsy. Her maiden voyage was on Coronation Day. The installation of the engines was finished at 8 pm on the night before, and the next morning the Herbert menage steamed downstream and anchored off the House of Commons. It is more than likely that this was the only party who saw the pageantry in complete comfort. Happy days as well as good salty adventure were experienced in the *Water Gipsy*. Her home waters were the Medway and the Thames as far as Whitstable. On one occasion she was run down in broad daylight by a Swedish two-thousand tonner in the Swale, but received no more than superficial damage. She was all set to venture to wider horizons when the Second World War intervened.

Sir Alan was proud of his many river friends. Like all watermen, he recalled hasty words given and taken, but he expressed great admiration for the competence, patience and good humour of the professional Thames watermen. As a Member of Parliament he brought to the notice of the Ministry of Food during the war some of the special rationing difficulties suffered by these men.

Some of Sir Alan's own adventures were the theme of some of his writings. *The Water Gipsies* contains much of what he saw and heard during his wanderings by canal and river. More personal experiences are found in *the Big Swim* and other works. But behind the mask of humour there is in all his writings about the river a deep affection for it.

To turn from literature to war, when, in common with most members of the Thames River Emergency Service, Sir Alan, then Mr A. P. Herbert, and his craft passed under the White Ensign: ship and crew entered the Thames Royal Naval Auxiliary Patrol. Through official and unofficial channels, HMS *Water Gipsy* became one of the most heavily armed vessels for her size and complement in the service. Only thirty-nine feet long and with a crew of three, she boasted two machine guns, three service rifles, three revolvers, one miniature rifle, one dozen hand grenades and two cutlasses.

It was during the blitz that Petty Officer Herbert opened fire from HMS *Water Gipsy* on low-flying enemy planes over Westminster. It was an historic occasion on two counts—it was probably the highest point up the Thames that a naval vessel had ever engaged the enemy, and it was probably the only time that a waterborne MP had taken an active part in the direct defence of the Houses of Parliament.

When parachute mines began to shower on the Port, Herbert and his craft were seconded to the Thames Minewatching and Mine Clearance Service. He gave much help in building up the organization whereby thousands of voluntary minewatchers turned out to plot the fall of these pests as soon as the sirens whined. But it was in the matter of mine-watching exercises that he

Petty Officer Sir Alan Herbert having trouble with the minewatching exercise balloon.

made his greatest contribution to defence of the Thames. Vital to training and sustained enthusiasm, these exercises demanded strictly accurate night positioning on the part of *Water Gipsy's* crew. Imagine a black winter's night on a blacked-out fast tide with perhaps a gale-driven curtain of rain to make it more difficult. Then visualize carrying out orders to be exactly on certain positions defined as so many cables on such and such bearings from a dozen different invisible landmarks scattered up or down five or six miles of the tideway. And each position had to be reached on a strict time schedule. But it was done every fortnight, and enemy minelaying in the Thames ceased.

When the enemy gave up minelaying in the Port of London, Herbert was directed to train Wren boat's crews. His young ladies, some sixty in number, received a sound training in seamanship and coastal navigation, passing out with a test which would not have disgraced the Board of Trade. It was during this period that the widow of a master mariner sent Herbert a sextant. He had hardly seen one before, but he threw himself into the study of blue-water navigation. I remember assisting at a long experiment, using an artificial horizon by means of which he triumphantly proved that he was in the vicinity of Westminster. Within a mere six months he had submitted to the Admiralty a novel navigational ready reckoner for survivors in ship's boats. And his well-known plan to rename the stars was inspired by his study of astro-navigation.

It was at about this period that the Admiralty created a new class of petty officers known as POPS (Petty Officers, Patrol Service). Herbert, who had often voiced his objection to the unfortunate title of the RNPS rating known as Second Hand was stung to verse by the threatened indignity of being labelled a "Pops".

The Savage Club saw a lot of the Navy as guests of Herbert during the war. On one occasion, when he was in the Chair, his guests ranged from two admirals down to a sub-lieutenant. He began his speech with: "It is not every petty officer who achieves the dream of all petty officers—to have his officers exactly where he wants them." On another occasion his guests were the two able seamen who comprised his crew. The hospitality of the Savage Club is well known and the two boys were made much of by the members. Later, one of the lads confessed that he had hitherto held revolutionary views, but that this visit had completely changed his political outlook. The capitalist class, he asserted, was first rate. Herbert wondered what the hard-working members of the Club would have said had they heard themselves described as capitalists.

Petty Officer Herbert was most punctilious about service relations with his officers, and a meeting was invariably accompanied by a fearful clash of heels and a sweeping naval salute, even if it was followed by an invitation to lunch in the House. Near VE Day, with post-war rehabilitation in mind, the Admiralty circulated a questionnaire about pre-war employment to all members of the Senior Service. The first question was: "How were you employed before the war?" To which Herbert replied: "Gainfully." The second question was: "Describe the nature of your work." Herbert's answer was simply: "Good."

When the time came for him to return to civilian life, he did not forget his comrades in the London River. One of his best speeches in the House protested against the Admiralty's refusal to grant the 1939–1945 Star to members of the Thames RNAP and Minesweeping Service who, under one of the most concentrated and sustained aerial attacks of the war, had done so much to keep the Port open. "The Admiralty", he said, "describes this mighty river . . . as 'sheltered' waters . . . I ask the Admiralty from what were these vessels 'sheltered'? They were not sheltered against bombs from above, or against mines below. . . The operation in which these services took part was not the Battle of Britain which lasted for two months, but the Battle of the Thames which lasted for twelve months." He was unsuccessful but his former shipmates remembered his speech with gratitude.

After the war, the *Water Gipsy* rode the tides beneath the window of Sir Alan's study. He never forgot his service in the Port of London. He will be long remembered in literary, stage, legal and Parliamentary circles, but the river remembers him as a fully paid-up Thamesman.

It was the stern of an outward-bound steamer seen from the King George V Dock pierhead that inspired me to include H. M. Tomlinson in my gallery of Thames-side characters. Tomlinson is to the Thames what Conrad is to the sailorman's sea.

There is a breath-trapping vastness about the lower Thames which defeats the cunning of the ordinary descriptive writer, however skilled; the river's moods change with the tide, and when the subject is seen only through the eyes it becomes more than the visiting writer can digest. To present a detailed and truthful portrait of the industrial Thames the writer must compare the scene before him with a score of other scenes filed in his mind. Few who write about the tideway have this necessary stock-in-trade; but Tomlinson describes the sprawling, shapeless, crowded life of the Thames of yesterday and of the longer past with unsurpassed fidelity and accuracy.

But Tomlinson goes much further than merely knowing his Thames. The art of writing is primarily the ability to think, on which is grafted by long training the faculty of expressing the thought in fresh and vigorous phrases. As a thinker, Tomlinson is profound and original. As a writer he instinctively side-steps cliches and stale metaphor. You may not agree with his philosophies, but you are never bored by his words. His work reveals wide reading, a deep appreciation of Thames's traditions and a passionate affection for the tidal stream "which is London's origin, life and circulation". For thinking, he gives us: "Let us reject the abominable heresy that the basis of history is bread, and butter if it can be got. If bread had been all that men were after they would have died out, or deserved to. Curiosity has performed greater miracles than love of gain; it has taken the gravest risks to gain nothing but a little more knowledge." As for descriptive writing, it would be hard to beat: "The chorus of shipwrights' mallets still went on in Blackwall Yard. In the docks at the bottom of the street could be seen the largesse of an abundant earth, mountains of coconuts, black pools on the quays from stove hogheads of molasses, and enough sugar to sweeten the sourest land."

In his well-known historical novel *Morning Light* he takes us back to the Thames in the days when the early haze of steam was beginning to obscure the seaways of sail and when the first fever spots of the Industrial Revolution were flushing the fair face of Merry England. The bold detail in his description of the Chartist movement, Wapping in the days of "Paddy's Goose", and the determination of most shipowners to ignore the disturbing alliance of iron with steam almost inspires the belief that Tomlinson actually lived in those transitional times. The secret behind the veracity of the scenes lies in his childhood. His father, a craftsman employed by the East and West India Docks Company, was a product of the roaring eighteen-forties and was therefore of Chartist and Nonconformist sympathies. It was through his father's eyes that Tomlinson saw and wrote about the self-righteous, smug and greedy ones who countenanced the grim sacrifice of women and babies to the new industrial Moloch; it is through those eyes that we see the pitiful sowing of the seed that has sprouted into the poisonous weed of irrational class-hatred.

In his book *London River* Tomlinson writes:

I remember an open space above the stairs [Blackwall] and a tavern, the Artichoke, looking over the river from its garden . . . We used to play there because it was forbidden. It was supposed to be dangerous. There, one summer evening, as the tide turned again to the sea, I stood to watch a barque cast off. She was bound out. The first lights were moving over the water, green, red and white planets confused in the mirk. The opposite shore had gone. We stared into a void. The barque was spectral as she moved away and then she dissolved. As we watched the dark where she had been we heard over the water her crew singing a departure chanty at the halliards.

The fruits of this and other early experiences are plucked in *Morning Light*, in which an imaginative and introspective boy sees the tideway romantically magnificent for the first time.

No one can love the Thames as Tomlinson loved it without also loving ships. And Tomlinson both loved and understood ships, qualities often unrelated. For a man who had never been a professional seaman the authenticity of his ship scenes and manoeuvres is at first sight amazing. But he began early, studying ships as boys today "collect" aircraft and motor cars, and listening to incessant ship shop in his home. Later, the talk was still of ships, for his in-laws represented most ranks in the merchant service from masters to sailmakers. In his youth he was employed in the

H. M. Tomlinson (centre) with Captain C. Cadge (left) and Philip Gibbs outside the war correspondents' headquarters at Amiens in the spring of 1917.

129

office of merchants in Leadenhall Street, and sailing cards of *Cutty Sark*, *Blackadder*, *Thermopylae* and many other flying beauties were collected by the impressionable lad. His duties took him frequently to the docks for mates' receipts and other shipping documents. Incidentally, it was that early office experience that provided him with the background for the opening chapters of his perhaps best-known book, *Gallions Reach*. But fate was by no means finished with the training of a nautical writer. When he went into Fleet Street, he spent many hours afloat—a whole December in a North Sea trawler, on naval manoeuvres and long passages in freighters. On one occasion he was taking passage in a cargo vessel which was beset by a gale; squalls of hurricane violence nearly sent her to the bottom in mid-Atlantic. One mate was taken ill and the other mate and the master became so exhausted that Tomlinson, with no ticket or other professional qualification, was left in charge of the bridge during a middle watch. One can now understand why he read Lecky for fun!

Much of this experience crystallized in *Gallions Reach*, in which the *Altair* sinks in the Indian Ocean. To make sure that his paper-and-ink ship manoeuvred correctly he was given permission by Lloyd's to examine the records of the *Snowdon Range*, battered almost to the point of foundering in 1912. He did not, of course, use this ship as his model but he made sure that what was done in his *Altair* had already been done at sea. Nevertheless, a maritime critic in an American high-brow magazine took exception to the way the *Altair* had been handled. But Tomlinson eventually had the satisfaction of hearing the famous Felix Reisenberg (late American master mariner and author of standard nautical textbooks) tell an audience of seamen and writers, including the critical critic, that he could find nothing wrong with the way Tomlinson handled a ship.

Space does not permit me to quote from *All Our Yesterdays*, with its memories of the Thames Iron Works before the London shipbuilding trade went north. But throughout his work the Thames runs like destiny. We who also love the river find inspiration in his words. Disciples he had a-plenty, but none can hope to outstrip the master, for H. M. Tomlinson will long stand as the supreme interpreter of the significance of the Thames tideway in London's life.

There the sun goes down into the smother of the ancient city. London puts out the fire of the westering sun before its due hour. That premonition ahead, immense and sombre, comes of the thoughts and desires of many generations of men, living and dead, good and bad. Nobody dare estimate how much is inimical in that ominous loom, shot with flames, beyond the ship's prow. London is ahead; and then one remembers the city's high tradition, and that its heritage is noble. One remembers the courage and endurance of its people when hope had all but gone; and cannot but feel that the dark scene has majesty, for it comes of the undying virtue of man's wayward but unceasing quest for good.

What more remains to be said?

Many other writers have fostered and interpreted the spirit of the river and sea. But it is almost a national calamity that radio and television have resulted in a complete generation to whom the stars of Dallas or Fawlty Towers mean more than Robinson Crusoe, Amyas Leigh or Captain Nemo. Most adults have at least nodding acquaintance with those old heroes who once so satisfactorily filled the leisure hours of boyhood, but for some sad and inexplicable reason the books of Captain Frederick Marryat now seem to be almost unknown to grown ups or children of today.

Captain Marryat died nearly a hundred and fifty years ago—in August, 1848. Although all his sea time was spent in ships of the Royal Navy, it seems that he was a Thames-sider by birth; his daughter stated that he was born at Westminster, but Christopher Lloyd proves, in his excellent biography (*Captain Marryat and the Old Navy*) that he was born in 1792 at Catharine Court on Tower Hill. So his first nautical impressions were undoubtedly gained from the merchant shipping in the Pool, only a few hundred yards away. Samuel Pepys's residence at Catharine Court and his association with the adjacent Navy Office, all swallowed up when construction of the PLA Building began in 1912, are perpetuated in the neighbouring Pepys Street. But no one now remembers Marryat's early connection with the home of British merchant shipping or that he was the son of a famous chairman of Lloyd's.

The popularity of Marryat's nautical works was maintained until the First World War. It was not until then that the average civilian came to realize the glamour of the modern Navy. Before then, *Frank Mildmay*, *Midshipman Easy* and other period stories by Marryat, all technically accurate and largely founded on his own varied and romantic career, satisfied the sea fever of boys to whom Trafalgar was still the last great sea fight; who had not yet thrilled at Jutland, Zeebrugge, or the Falklands. A second world war, ringing with immortal names like Dunkirk, River Plate and Crete, may be the reason for the final eclipse of Marryat and other contemporary writers about the old-style Navy of the days of sail.

Marryat will always be of value to the nautical historian, for he faithfully records a transitional period of the Navy at the end of the Napoleonic wars. He was himself in action more than a hundred times. His conscientious application to the dull and difficult duty of maintaining anti-smuggling patrols in the Channel was on a par with his courageous exposure of the inefficiency and evils of the Press Gang. The first-named duty earned for him the dislike of the smugglers; the second incurred the displeasure, much worse in effect, of the Admiralty. His last important sea service was the command of the naval forces at the First Burmese War. Most lasting of his work was the invention of a merchant service flag-signalling code which eventually provided a basis for the first International Code.

His greatest and best-known boys' book, *Masterman Ready*, was inspired by irritation at the impossibilities and absurdities perpe-trated in *The Swiss Family Robinson*. Equally popular was *The Children of the New Forest*. He shared with his friend Charles Dickens an absorbing love of children which mellowed his vanity during his hey-day and softened the irascibility of his declining years. But above all else Marryat was a seaman, a distinction of which he was more proud than of his claim to authorship.

The centenary and a half of a nautical writer about whom Joseph Conrad wrote: "He is the enslaver of youth, not by the false glamour of presentation, but by the heroic quality of his own unique temperament" is surely worthy of some form of memorial. And what more appropriate place than the ancient hill where he was born, close to the noble river which first fired him with his undying love of ships and the sea.

The two things creating the greatest unrest in the heart of mankind, love and the sea, have had more words poured out about them than any other subjects within human knowledge. An attempt to name the greatest writer of love stories would without doubt provoke a storm of dissension. But most discriminating seamen and sea lovers will agree that Joseph Conrad was the supreme interpreter of the minds and lives of the men who served the sea in the days of sail.

There is no doubt that Conrad also loved the Thames. He had no ties there, but he deliberately chose London as his home port and lived there between voyages. Prior to joining the famous passenger and wool clipper *Torrens* as chief officer he was for a short spell the manager of a Thames-side warehouse. *Torrens* discharged in the London Dock, and up to comparatively recent times Conrad was well remembered by at least one of the dock officials on the North Quay.

To those unacquainted with his works some facts about his career are necessary properly to appreciate his genius and his impressions of the Port of London in the days of the zenith and decline of square-rigged ships. He was born in 1857 in the Ukraine of Polish parents as Teodor Josef Konrad Korzeniowski. Although living amongst a people almost completely unfamiliar with the sea,

Joseph Conrad, who wrote with affection about the Port of London in the days of sail.
Courtesy: Museum in Dockland

Conrad determined at an early age not only to become a sailor, but also to serve under the Red Ensign. How he attained this ambition is a story too long to be included in this book, but by 1878 he had had much sea experience and was in that school of many fine seamen, the British North Sea coasting trade.

In 1886 he became a naturalized British subject, soon afterwards acquiring his Master's Certificate. The same year he wrote his first story, *The Black Mate*, which was unsuccessful in a

133

competition organized by *Tit-Bits*. For some time he continued to sail the seas, noting subconsciously with the born writer's microscopic eye the men and events to be used later in his writings. In 1889 he began writing his first novel, *Almeyer's Folly*. In *A Personal Record* Conrad described the "opaline mist" over London on the morning that he started this novel in his lodgings near Vauxhall Bridge, and how this atmospheric effect was due to the proximity of the Thames. From that point his mind travelled to the similar mist overlying a Bornean river where he had met Almeyer. Then, inspired by the recollection, he began his writing career.

Thus Conrad's first serious attempt at writing was attributable to London River. *Almeyer's Folly* was not finished until 1894, and the manuscript suffered many vicissitudes, including a trip from the Royal Victoria Dock to Rouen and another journey to the Congo, but it was one of his most successful books. Conrad was a genius in two spheres; choosing a profession in which he had no backing of national tradition or family precept, he rose to the front rank of a foreign service, and he reached the top of another profession by writing exemplary prose in a foreign language learned in the forecastles of merchant ships.

The Faithful River, one of the essays in *The Mirror of the Sea*, expresses much of his affection for the Thames. It includes a description of the river as Conrad imagined it appeared to the commander of the first Roman galley to visit London. He wrote: "The estuary of the Thames is not beautiful; it has no noble features, no romantic grandeur of aspect, no smiling geniality; but it is wide open, spacious, inviting, hospitable at the first glance with a strange air of mysteriousness which lingers about it to this very day." We may truthfully add "And even today".

Conrad maintained that the Thames was the only great commercial stream in the British Isles open to romantic feeling, owing to the fact that factories did not stretch along its banks to the very sea. If Thames-side development continues at its present pace, this romantic atmosphere will not cling to the estuary much longer. But his description of the outward-bound traffic holds good, I venture to prophesy, for all time: "On the imposing expanse of the great estuary the traffic of the port where so much of the world's work and the world's thinking is being done becomes insignificant, scattered, streaming away in thin lines of ships stringing themselves out into the eastern quarter through the various navigable channels of which the Nore lightship [now replaced by a navigation buoy] marks the divergence." He amplified this description with "They follow each other, going very close by the Essex shore. Such as the beads of a rosary told by businesslike shipowners for the greater profit of the world, they slip out one by one into the open."

Of the approach to Gravesend Reach he wrote: "That hint of

loneliness, that soul of the sea which had accompanied her [the ship] as far as the Lower Hope Reach, abandons her at the turn of the first bend above." The industrial reaches between London Bridge and the Royal Albert Dock are described as "to other watersides of river ports what a virgin forest would be to a garden" and summed up as "the waterside of watersides".

Much of *The Faithful River* deals with the docks. There is in it an amusing description of how a berthing master warned Conrad, just in time, to haul round the topgallant yards of his ship before they broke the windows of the quayside warehouse. In this essay, too, we find an unexpected championship of the old dock companies. They had lacked, Conrad maintained, industrial backing, and he contended that the development of the Port had been worthy of its dignity. He described the dirt and horror of the docks of some unnamed northern port and then went on: "One thing, however, may be said for the docks of the Port of London on both sides of the river: for all the complaints of their insufficient equipment, of their obsolete rules, of failure (they say) in the matter of quick despatch, no ship need ever issue from their gates in a half-fainting condition!" The obsolete rules were probably those ordering the extinction at an early hour of all fire and light in ships in dock, described by Conrad in the novel *Chance*. He admitted that the docks of the Thames are ugly, but he added "romance has lived too long upon this river not to have thrown a mantle of glamour upon its banks."

Fog, of course, was an arch-enemy to Conrad, as it is to all seamen, but he even romanticized Thames fog with: "Through the long and glorious tale of years of the river's strenuous service to its people, these are its only breathing times."

In Captivity begins with a description of ships caged in dock, in which Conrad's true sailor character revolted at the inaction. He wrote, too, of a common sight in the South West India Dock: a line, a quarter-of-a-mile in length, of lovely clippers berthed on the north side with spars dwarfing the sheds, jib-booms extended far over the shore and white and gold figureheads overhanging the quayside. Those were the ships, he sighed, which, after having braved so many tempests, "have been blown off the face of the sea by a puff of steam."

Initiation tells of the exhibition of the art of shipbuilding and the art of figurehead carving seen throughout the year in "the open-air gallery of the New South Dock". The crowds which Conrad met at the dock line terminus at Fenchurch Street were "in jerseys and pilot cloth mostly, and had the air of being more conversant with the times of high-water than with the times of trains".

Another of Conrad's books, *A Personal Record*, contains some revealing pictures of the Board of Trade examinations for masters and mates held in those days in St Katharine Dock House. During one of these examinations Conrad was placed in command of an imaginary ships on which the examiner inflicted one by one the manifold dangers of the sea. As fast as Conrad extricated his ship from one misadventure another mishap threatened. Conrad, in desperation, at last decided to let go his anchors. But when the examiner informed him that one of the anchor cables had parted, he replied that in spite of tailing the heaviest hawser on board on the end of the chain the second cable would probably go and that he could do no more. "Nothing more to do, eh?" asked the examiner. "No, sir. I could do no more." Whereupon the examiner reminded him that he could always say his prayers as a last resource. These examinations at St Katharine Dock House are also referred to in *Chance*, and it is more than probable that Conrad and other embryo masters and mates took test bearings of adjacent warehouse roofs through the windows of the room where the PLA Staff had their club before the war. In *Chance*, too, is a description of the Shipping Office in the same building, now demolished after blitz damage, formerly known to seamen as "The Chain Locker".

In *The Heart of Darkness* Conrad invites us with a magnificent gesture to look at all those things, tangible and intangible, which have made Thames "The River":

> Forthwith a change came over the waters, and the serenity became less brilliant but more profound. The old river in its broad reach rested unruffled at the decline of day, after ages of good service done to the race that peopled its banks, spread out in the tranquil dignity of a waterway leading to the uttermost parts of the earth. We looked at the venerable stream not in the vivid flush of the short day that comes and departs for ever, but in the august light of abiding memories. And, indeed, nothing is easier for a man who has, as the phrase goes, "followed the sea" with reverence and affection, than to evoke the great spirit of the past upon the lower reaches of the Thames. The tidal current runs to and fro in its unceasing service, crowded with memories of men and ships it has borne to the rest of home or to the battles of the sea. It had known and served all the men of whom the nation is proud, from Sir Francis Drake to Sir John Franklin, knights all, titled and untitled—the great knights errant of the sea. It had borne all the ships whose names are like jewels flashing in the night of time, from the *Golden Hind* returning with her round flanks full of treasure, to be visited by the Queen's Highness and thus pass out of the gigantic tale, to the *Erebus* and *Terror* bound on other conquests—and that never returned.

After his sea-going experiences Conrad renewed his acquaintance with the Thames when he lived at Stanford-le-Hope, and here and there in his many other books are references to the docks, the river, seamen in the port and the Dock Companies' servants. Throughout his work Conrad exhibits the quiet restraint and self-discipline of the quarterdeck, but he was nevertheless a romantic. This is, of course, a sin in these days of literary cynicism, but how could the arena in which man for countless centuries has pitted himself against the most elemental forces of nature be truly described except in a romantic vein? Conrad has put the soul of the sailor, the very soul of the sea, into his writings, and the Thames, receiving twice a day the embrace of salt water, shares in his devotion.

We paid proper respect to South Devon Wharf when we passed it in the first chapter: the place where William Wymark Jacobs lived and the background for many of his yarns. He spent most of his youth at this insalubrious spot, his father being wharf manager. He was a lonely boy, for, decently educated at private schools, he found little congenial company or amusement in the roaring sailortown of Wapping in his day. Like many other lonely souls, he found companionship in his imagination, which in the course of time became focused upon the colourful harbour life sprawling round his doorstep.

When he was twenty years of age, he entered the Civil Service Savings Bank Branch. But to a man of imagination brought up beside the London River, it was inevitable that brown spritsails and steamer smoke would continually obliterate the stiff dry figures in his ledgers. In 1899 he forsook the furtherance of thrift among the masses for the more congenial world of imagination and romance.

The majority of his yarns are set in or around the river. But he had no flair for descriptive writing; the opening paragraph usually bluntly announces that the background is Wapping, Limehouse or Gravesend, and beyond these bald statements there is hardly a single passage in his works about the rich industrial frieze of Thames-side or about the kaleidoscope of ships, craft and cargo movement before his tide-washed door. Jacobs's success was his grasp of the fact that most readers are more interested in people than in places or things. He still stands as the supreme interpreter of the robust wit and pungent humour of the tideway.

He was happiest when writing about the longshoremen he knew so well. His stories set in barges or coasters ring slightly false, and many technical slips betray his lack of first-hand experience in nautical matters. But perhaps, when night falls, the spirit of Bill, the night watchman, emerges from the new development, ready to spin another yarn.

A portrait gallery of Thames-side writers cannot fail to be enriched by the inclusion of a group of present-day artists who find their inspiration along the tidal Thames.

The Wapping Group of artists was very British in its

beginnings, for it evolved and grew to its present stature with a minimum of planning and with little more knowledge about its conception than Topsy had about hers. All the original members belonged to the Langham Sketching Club, London's oldest art club, founded in 1838. The Langham does not meet during the summer months, and these members, in ones and twos, made it a practice to take the myriad features of the Thames as subjects for their art during the Langham close season. They first concentrated on the Wapping area, but today they range both banks of the whole of the tidal Thames. A remark, so casual that no one now remembers who made it, eventually led to an inaugural supper at The Prospect of Whitby in May, 1947; and the Wapping Group, already half-grown, found itself officially born.

Record of a day's painting in dockland. Courtesy: The Wapping Group

The general public knew little about the group or its work until August, 1947, when the Port of London Authority provided space in their head offices for the group's first exhibition, "The Spirit of London River". Opened by Sir Alan Herbert, the exhibition immediately attracted the attention of the City's shipping community. Four of the exhibition pictures were televised in the BBC Picture Page feature. The clannish Thames-side dwellers and workers gave guarded approval to artists who by the magic of vision and brush transmuted their mundane daily sights into things of wonder and beauty; they appreciated the deft capture of fleeting colours in the sky and on the water which most of them are too inarticulate to describe. The second "Spirit of London River" exhibition was held at the PLA head offices a year later. Opened by Sir John Anderson, later Lord Waverley, it convinced Thames-side that the Wapping Group knew what it was painting. And full approval by Thames-side is no mean achievement, as others have sometimes found. Since then the Group has held an exhibition each year. The Wapping Group's "Friday evening on the riverside" is now a well-known summer feature of the tideway.

Like all Thames-side worthies, most members of the Group have had adventures, some of which are recorded in pencil and paint in their official annals. On one occasion the Group made a trip from the upper docks to Gravesend in an outward-bound vessel, sketching the passing waterfront. When the time came to leave the ship, they transferred to a tug via a rope ladder. Loaded with the implements of their art, the rope ladder was a bit difficult, and one member, even when confronted with the possibility of an enforced sea voyage, refused to attempt the descent. The picture which records the incident in the annals shows him being ignominiously lowered to the tug in a coal basket.

When the artists set up their easels in Wapping, Rotherhithe or other waterside districts where the young Thames-sider abounds, each one invariably becomes the centre of an interested crowd of boys and girls. The members of the Wapping Group consider that boys are better art critics than girls; the former do not crowd the artist too closely, and many of them, after the usual opening remarks—"Isn't it smashing?" or "Are you an artist?" or "Do you get money for your pictures?"—keep quiet and are genuinely interested.

One member painting on the foreshore at an early hour was cut off by the tide. He reached the bank wet and muddy to the knees and clutching gear under one arm and an unfinished canvas under the other. With a strange pattern of vermilion and blue on the side of his coat, he sadly watched a favourite brush and other paraphernalia float outward bound.

Mud, rain, fog and transport difficulties have been braved in
the efforts of the Wapping Group to stimulate a wider knowledge
of and admiration for the tidal Thames and its great port. Whistler
expressed the appeal of the Thames for all artists with: "When the
evening mist clothes the riverside with poetry, as with a veil, and
the tall chimneys become campanili and the warehouses are palaces
in the night . . ." And we who have seen poetry in the westering
sun in Sea Reach, in a long ribbon of funnel smoke trailing over a
waterside Essex marsh or in the rigid canvas of a barge driving past
a pierhead in a February gale know that these men are seekers
after things worth while; that to them the blind materialism of a
selfish age is so much dross.

★

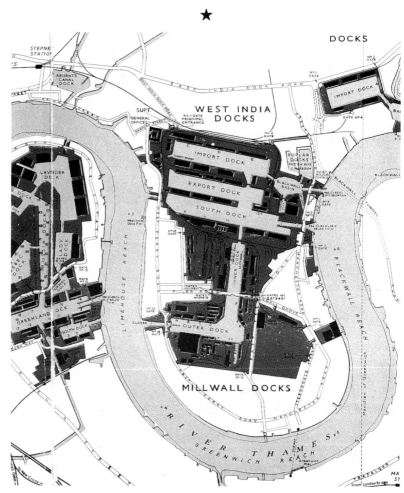

*Port of London
Authority, plan of West
India and Millwall
Docks.*

Upper and Middle Docks   12

THE IMPOUNDED docks of the Port of London were inspired by plans to avoid tidal power and thefts. As early as the Roman occupation, docks for the loading and discharge of ships had been created at Queenhithe and Billingsgate, but they were little more than berths which dried out at low water. As ships grew bigger, simple tidal basins were built, first at Rotherhithe and later at Blackwall, where ships could be equipped and fitted out. But in the main, bigger ships, too large to sit on low-water mud, had to moor in midstream. With the growth of oversea trade in Elizabethan times, the congestion in the upper tidal reaches, notably in the Pool of London, became acute. For long periods, smaller vessels lay idle, queuing for berths alongside the inadequate number of quays, while the larger ships awaited craft for the overside discharge of cargo.

This marine scrum gave rise to a great flood of organized piracy. Ships were raided, sometimes by armed gangs; corrupt ship's officers allowed petty thieves on board; equally corrupt deck hands hove pieces of cargo overboard to be retrieved by accomplices from the mud; in some cases, ships were actually seized and towed away to a quieter berth where they could be stripped.

The solution was found in the building of enclosed docks in which ships could lie alongside in tide-free water while their cargoes would be protected by massive walls guarded day and night by the dock company's own police. The first such haven was the West India Docks, opened in 1802 on the north bank near the end of Blackwall Reach. At first it consisted of two separate basins, the Import and Export Docks, linked by a tidal dock. In 1803, the Corporation of London (then conservators of the tidal river) built a canal across the peninsula formed by Limehouse, Greenwich and Blackwall Reaches, thus creating the Isle of Dogs. But short cuts sometimes cut short, and the canal was not a commercial success. In 1829 it was bought by the West India Dock Company and became the South Dock, parallel with the Export Dock. The Millwall Dock was added to the group in 1868. The whole complex of four docks was joined by cuttings and given a new entrance lock in 1929.

Legislation permitting the building of the docks gave the company a twenty-one-year monopoly for handling all West Indian cargo entering the port and, although the monopoly had long since expired, this type of cargo still predominated there until the docks were closed. The West India Docks had one very impressive feature—nearly three-quarters of a mile of Georgian warehouses which were both decorative and functional. Originally built as nine separate blocks, they were eventually joined to provide one of the finest industrial façades in Britain. Vast quantities of West Indian cane sugar were stored here. With true Georgian belief in the permanence of the status quo, these warehouses were built to last for centuries. But at the beginning of the nineteenth century West Indian sugar was imported in hogsheads which had to be handled manually. As a result these huge containers could only be stowed two high. And the warehouse ceilings were accordingly low. When bagged sugar began to supplant the hogsheads, economical stowage was hampered by the low ceilings. Much of this line of buildings was destroyed during the blitz. What remains has been taken over by the Docklands Development Corporation, but the façades are guarded by a preservation order.

The much publicized Canary Wharf is rising on the site of the former West India Docks Rum Quay. There was something about the old quay that lent it a little of the atmosphere of a boat builder's yard; an air of directed activity and honest work mellowed by old tradition. There was also a flavour of that adventurous past of which rum, above all stimulants, can boast; a whiff of the sea, the roar of high winds in Jamaica, the frowzy pirates of the Gulf Keys, bandannas, seamen in earrings and fancy pants.

The Rum Quay was nearly 140 years old when it was destroyed. It still had much of the venerable routine of other days, for, until the bottling stage, chromium-plated time savers could do little to help in the sampling, blending, fining, clearing, colouring, racking and necessary cooperage carried out by the skilled warehouse staff.

The Rum Quay knew twenty-three different types of rum. Some are colourless, others range from straw colour to dark brown. Rum was by no means the monopoly of the West Indies, for most of the sugar-cane-producing countries of the world sent rum to the Rum Quay. Rank after rank of puncheons (surely the most sonorous of all the names in the hierarchy of casks) would arrive and be set out on the quay. They were made of oak and the normal stock was about 15,000. Customs Officers would move along the ranks, juggling with slide rules and hydrometers. With a distressing lack of faith in human nature, these officers, the real power at the old Quay, kept the water supply and colouring matter under lock, and supervised sampling and any other operations carried out by the staff on behalf of the importers. Over the ranks of waiting puncheons stretched a roof which in 1851 had been a covered entrance to the Crystal Palace Exhibition.

In the vaults below the Quay, because of the inflammable nature of the spirit, polished tin reflectors were used to catch light from the windows, until the introduction of electricity made it easier to read identity marks on the puncheons.

Another floor at the Quay was devoted to the vats, brooding silently here and there like something out of "Doctor Who". Made of English oak, their capacities ranged from a few hundred gallons to the largest, holding 7,800 gallons. Rum containing large quantities of suspended matter had to be cleared; it would be poured into a vat through an aperture in the floor above. Milk might be added, and within a short time precipitation was complete, and the rum could be drawn off quite clear, or as the trade termed it, bright. One wonders if some old planter discovered this process by adding crude rum to the milk diet ordered by his doctor. Other vats were used for blending, and the different rums would be "roused" by a mechanical impeller.

Outside the trade, a legend once current told of Rum Quay workers and others employed in spirit vaults becoming fuddled with the fumes. It was not true. A headache was the worst effect of living with a lake of hard liquor. When the Rum Quay burned*, the puncheons exploded and burst into rivers of fire. With it burned a century and a half of tradition. The trade became centred elsewhere, and when the Navy's lower deck became virtually teetotal imports declined.

The sugar which first arrived in the hogsheads and later in bags was beginning to be imported in bulk when these docks were closed. The other main import at the West India Docks was hardwood with strange-sounding names such as gaboon, jarrah, padauk, sapele, as well as the more familiar mahogany, ebony, greenheart and teak. The huge baulks were formerly moved and piled by horsedrawn trolleys, but later by gantries and travelling cranes.

In the adjoining Millwall Docks, the theme was grain in bulk, signified by the towering Central Granary. This huge rambling building of conveyors, shutes and silos, was perpetually shrouded in a fog of grain dust. Independent dockside flour mills also took bulk deliveries.

Before the war, square-rigged ships and barques sometimes berthed there at the end of the so-called Australian Grain Race. This was the last refuge of the almost extinct commercial windjammer. The lofty masts and spars of *Archibald Russell, Herzogin Cecilie, Lingard, Loch Linnhe, Abraham Rydberg*, and others which had seen better days, occasionally brought a touch of romance to the scene.

The Thames on Fire by L. M. Bates (Terence Dalton, Ltd)

About half a mile east of the West India Docks was the little East India group, built by the Honourable East India Company and opened in 1806 with a monopoly for handling all London-bound cargo from China and the East Indies. It consisted of an Export Dock, built on the site of the eighteenth-century Brunswick Dock, and an Import Dock, both served by a tidal basin.

Even before the war these docks were slowly decaying; the decline in Empire had left them stranded, too small and too old to be worth modernizing. They still harboured ocean-going and coastal vessels, and some eastern cargo was still dealt with, but the group was on its way out.

However behind the shabby warehouse walls lay a story unsurpassed elsewhere in the port. The story of sail was told here, first by the stately East Indiamen, then the Blackwall Frigates and lastly the clippers; famous and beautiful ships such as Captain Renaut's *Crusader*, the *Pericles*, *Mermerus*, *Brilliant* and *Lord Warden*. From these ramshackle basins had sailed, as Captain Renaut told, many pioneers intent on colonizing new lands.

In the library of HM Customs I found the sailing lists of the *Lord William Bentinck* and the *Regulus*, which left these docks in

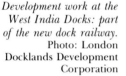

Development work at the West India Docks: part of the new dock railway.
Photo: London Docklands Development Corporation

1841 for Wellington and Port Phillip respectively. The former ship, only 443 tons, carried 234 emigrants "equal to 162½ adults", and the latter of 369 tons (little bigger than a barge) embarked "forty-three souls equal to 30⅔ adults". The fractions were the result of calculating the relative space taken up by adults and children: most of the emigrants had large families.

At Wapping on the north bank, a little below Tower Bridge, was a rambling series of lagoons, leading one from the other; this complex was the London Docks. Nearby upstream were the St Katharine Docks. The former was opened in 1805; the St Katharine group followed in 1828. Together they formed the port's principal storage centre. The comparatively narrow internal roads were lined by grim fortress-like warehouses which reflected the accent on security. But slight relief was provided by the occasional display of an ammonite, left in the plinths by the masons. These docks berthed small ships in Continental trades, coasters and barges. The great bulk of the wealth behind these impregnable walls had been barged up from larger ships that had discharged in the deeper docks downstream. Before the war, the warehousing of imports was all-important.

Wool, wines and spirits, drugs, iodine, gums, rubber, ivory, mercury, shells, spices, tortoiseshell, essential oils, perfumes, coffee, cocoa, dried fruits and canned goods, these and many other commodities had their own special fastnesses with staff skilled in processing on behalf of the importers. Most storage had its distinctive smell, in some cases its own stink. On the bare stone floors, one could see the real nitty-gritty of international trade. The staff casually spoke of what were in those little-travelled days exotic ends of the earth.

Modern packaging could have found inspiration in the wrappers and containers, for primitive producers, not yet sophisticated by modern electronics, used what nature had given them. Aloes, for instance, were poured in liquid form into monkey skins and allowed to harden into gruesome objects. Civet, exuded by the civet cat and used as a fixative for high-class perfumes, used to arrive from Abyssinia (Ethiopia) in such small consignments that it was contained in plugged buffalo horns. Some gums came inside bamboo canes, while the ubiquitous jerrycan was a heaven-sent container for all sorts of surprises.

Both these dock groups suffered heavily during the blitz. During the last few years, the scenario has changed out of all knowledge under the Docklands Development schemes. One of the St Katharine Dock basins has become a haven where the old Nore Lightship and other superannuated vessels are displayed. Warehouses have been demolished or adapted and waterways realigned.

All the warehouses had their own staff of semi-wild cats which waged war on the rats. They had an official allowance of meat and milk. Sometimes, a cat, bored with chasing rats, would select a vessel to its liking and make a voyage—perhaps to Australia or the Far East—returning in due course to its former employment in a dock warehouse.

When the warehousemen, usually with little book learning, spoke of the particular commodity in their care, they became unusually coherent, boldly expressing opinions based on a of lifetime knowledge. The commodity markets relied heavily on their skill in sorting, grading, sampling and garbling (sorting sound from unsound).

London had for long been the world's wool market, and at the London Docks some thirty acres of storage space were allocated to about 200,000 bales from Australia, New Zealand, South Africa and South America. About eight acres on the top floor of the wool warehouses were set aside for the display of bales before the six annual auction sales held at the Wool Exchange. The bales were cut open and prospective buyers from several different parts of the world would examine the wool.

My friend here, the foreman, would talk learnedly about fleeces, slipe wool (taken from a dead animal), scoured wool (its natural lanoline extracted) and greasy wool (in its natural state). But he could be rather basic in his exposition. On one occasion, I had taken a class of high-school girls to his warehouse; they were led by a rather snooty mistress. The foreman went through his routine and then showed them a fleece which, largely consisting of wool, also had a large quantity of goat's hair. "Oh," asked the mistress, scenting material for a biology lesson, "how did that come about?" To my embarrassment, he leered at her. "Ain't you never had a night out on the tiles?" he replied.

London was also then the world market for ivory. In the days before safari parks were invented, the Ivory Floor at the London and St Katharine Docks reflected wildlife in far places. Great elephant tusks and rhinoceros horns were laid out in orderly rows, ready for inspection prior to the next auction sale. My friend, Mr Yates, the foreman, asserted that some came from the execution of rogue elephants, and some were found ivory, but few were sportsmen's trophies. Elephant poaching was not then a problem. On instructions from the importers, he would set his staff sawing up the different parts of a tusk; one part would be sold to the makers of bangles, another part would go to the makers of billiard balls, other sections would be made into piano keys or curios. Even the dust from the saw cuts would be sold.

Elephant tusks are as sensitive as human teeth, and Mr Yates would shine a torch down the hollow part and show the six or seven feet of decay that had caused a beast to become a rogue. Grooves in a tusk would indicate a tusk having been sawn back and forth against a tree to alleviate the pain. Deeper ridges would show where a crocodile had tried a bite on the tusk of an animal lying dead in a swamp.

The Ivory Floor also handled regular consignments of huge mammoth tusks taken from animals preserved in the frozen soil of Siberia. But they proved of little commercial value; billiard balls made from them did not run true, and piano keys turned yellow. Rhinoceros horn, merely hair matted with a natural glue, usually went to the Far East, where it is regarded as an aphrodisiac. Occasionally the Ivory Floor was brightened by the splendour of a narwhal horn. The six feet or more of pure ivory in spiralling furrows had a medieval fairytale aura; the other name of the Narwhal is sea unicorn.

The official trade in imported ivory began to wilt under the post-war competition of plastics, but the official export of tusks gathered momentum as African natives, trained during the war in the use of automatic weapons, began poaching. The threat to elephant herds became so great that a ban was placed on the international sale of ivory. This, coupled with the closing of the London and St Katharine Docks, killed the ivory trade so far as London was

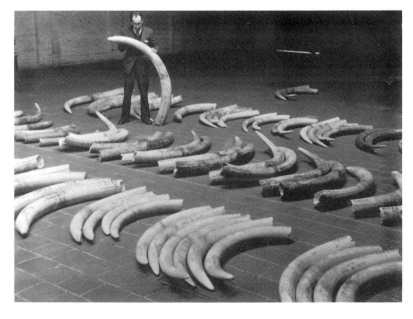

Ivory being laid out for display at the Ivory Floor, St Katharine Dock, prior to an auction sale.
Courtesy: Museum in Dockland

147

concerned. But although the Ivory Floor went out of business, tradition, which dies hard in Dockland, has named a part of modern dockland development "Ivory House".

Among the many cargoes featured in the long story of London's River wine has always been prominent. First imported by the Roman forces in Britain, it arrived in amphorae. By medieval times the Bordeaux wine trade with London was so important that it provided legal hypotheses for the Rule of Olèron, foundation of much of the International Law of the Seas. When the Plantagenets ruled part of France, the annual wine fleet used to leave the Thames with woollens for Bordeaux and return with tuns of wine. The tun was a very big cask taking up much space in a ship's hold, and it became the standard for modern shipboard space measurement, the register shipping ton of 100 cubic feet. And it is possible that the term migrated ashore to become the tonne avoirdupois. This Thames wine trade became centred at the London Docks. For more than a hundred years, imported wine was stored in vaults beneath the wool warehouses. Outside on the Gauging Ground scores of casks usually sat in orderly rows for their contents to be gauged by HM Customs.

In 1951 I went to the Crescent Vault at the London Docks to bid farewell to Mr W. T. Popkin, about to retire after forty-six years' service. He had entered the ranks of the London and India Dock Company in 1905 and soon afterwards became an apprentice cooper. Those were the days when horse-drawn road traffic and sailing ships were still fighting a vigorous rearguard action against the encroachments of machines; the days when skilled craftsmen were still encouraged to take pride in their work.

Mr Popkin told me about the ordeal of passing out of his seven years' apprenticeship and the traditional rites which were still practised. A half-completed cask was taken, still warm from the fire in which its staves had been bent, and the novice was dropped inside. The hoops were then driven on and the cask, still containing the apprentice, was rolled up and down the cobbled yard. He was then christened with a bucket or two of water and stirred with a mop, finally emerging a fully fledged cooper.

"Sucking the monkey", illicit drinking from casks of liquor, was then not uncommon, but he maintained that his generation was much more law-abiding. One of his duties in those days was to prepare casks in which vintage sherry was sent for a long voyage for the benefit of its health. When it returned to the Thames it was taken into the vaults again for subsequent bottling.

In the course of nearly half a century's experience he had seen the Empire wine trade grow from a neglected trickle to a much-appreciated torrent. He had seen the locked safety lanterns in the Brandy Vaults, as well as the oil-burning torches in the less

Inflammable wine vaults, superseded by the electric hand lamp. But he had seen no change in the tools of his craft, for the weirdly shaped weapons used by coopers—the heading knife for bevelling the heads of casks, the adze, chive and croze for trimming chimbs (the rims at the ends of casks), the axe, backing and hollowing knives for dressing staves, and the bickiron for riveting the hoops—had altered no more during his years of service than they had for many centuries before he came to the wine trade. Mr Popkin retired as Vault Keeper at the London Dock. In his charges were about 80,000 casks of wines and spirits (about five million gallons) stored in twenty-five acres of dock vaults.

Alleged to have been built by Napoleonic prisoners of war, these vast caverns were stuffed with hogsheads, pipes, barrels and casks of liquor from many different countries. Every item was inscribed with registered marks and numbers, incised with a scribing iron, a traditional implement rather like an old-fashioned

The wine gauging ground, London Docks, circa 1950, showing casks laid out for gauging. The entrance to the Crescent Wine Vaults can be seen in the background.
Courtesy: Museum in Dockland

149

tin opener. Within a gloom relieved only by an occasional gas jet regulated to keep the vault temperature at a steady sixty degrees Fahrenheit, with footsteps deadened by a thick carpet of sawdust, the roof thick with fungus formed by exhalations from wine, these vaults had something of a Tolkien-like atmosphere.

Important visitors used to be taken to the Crescent Vault where the dock superintendent would officially assure them that he had permission from the wine trade to give them a taste, and he would produce a time-worn tasting order. Then Mr Popkin would select a cask, and one of his coopers would give two or three shrewd blows with his flogger (mallet) on each side of the shive (bung), causing it to jump out. A valinche (long metal tube like a laboratory pipette) would be plunged into the cask and withdrawn full of wine to charge the glasses. During the latter half of the nineteenth century and right up to the last war many British and foreign royals and other celebrities visited these vaults.

In the less sophisticated days of Mr Popkin's service, the spirit of Dickens triumphantly survived austerity, and the approach of Christmas regularly sent the Press to the vaults for interviews and pictures.

Before we leave the Wine Vaults, mention must be made of a corollary to the use of the scribing iron. Blitz damage to a warehouse revealed a beam on which a doodler early in the last century had used his scribing iron to record: "Lord Nelson dyed [*sic*] in victory 1805".

To bring the Thames wine story up to date: in 1959 the first bulk-wine berth was built at the London Docks. It was equipped with reinforced glass-lined tanks with a total capacity of 200,000 gallons. The plastic pipes and non-frothing electric pumps could discharge tank barges or bulk-wine ships at some 9,000 gallons an hour, a river of wine not hitherto met outside legendary celebrations. The wine could likewise be pumped from the berth to road tankers. Two hundred thousand gallons imported by former traditional methods would have needed about four thousand casks with high labour costs for the manhandling involved. At the new berth, three men controlled all operations by push button.

With the closure of the London Docks in 1969 under the Docklands Development scheme, a new bulk-wine berth was built at the West India Docks. When that dock, too, closed for redevelopment, the berth, reduced in size, was leased to a private importer. At the time of writing, wine is discharged elsewhere in the Thames and delivered by road tanker to the berth, but it is hoped that the entry and discharge of bulk-wine ships direct may again become possible.

Closely associated with the London and St Katharine Docks as a port storage centre were the vast rambling PLA warehouses in Cutler Street, behind Houndsditch in the City. They were built in 1782 by the Honourable East India Company and had been inherited, with the East Anglia Docks, by the PLA (sold for redevelopment in 1971).

Here was a treasure house of strange and beautiful things and intriguing smells. The smells were mainly found at the Drug Floor. Most pleasant was the aromatic odour of vanilloes; this product of a plant of the orchid family looks rather like a long black slug with a coating of fine crystals. Strangely enough, ambergris and civet, the bases of most good perfumes, have smells almost impossible to describe. The former has something approaching a faintly fishy odour and the latter a revolting smell like nothing else on earth. An innocuous vegetable extract, looking like a more than usually embarrassed Dutch cheese, bore the fearsome name of Dragon's Blood. And there were the gruesome monkey skins filled with aloes, already mentioned.

In the carpet section, there were humble coverings designed for some suburban floor, and eastern rainbows imprisoned in gossamer fit for the haunches of what the crossword clues call an oriental potentate. Most of the consignments were only pausing at Cutler Street before setting out again as re-exports. But in those days, before air travel had stripped the romance of far away, the most intriguing sight was the little heap of desert sand and camel droppings which frequently fell out when a bale was first opened. What a tale this told of shambling camel trains, lonely oases and the age-old background of desert trade routes!

Legislation stopped the import of certain plumage, but there was an Ostrich-feather Floor at Cutler Street. And while lady visitors admired the beautiful, long, swaying plumes once destined maybe for plebeian hats on Hampstead Heath, but at that time more likely for beauty choruses, male visitors would make for the Cigar Floor. But both sexes would look with astonishment at the Curio Floor. Ink cannot do justice to the beauty of centuries-old porcelain, to the hideous grimace of an ivory fisherman, or to the impudent twinkle in the eye of the leading elephant of a tiny line crossing an ivory bridge only three inches long. One of the exhibits in a small Cutler Street museum told a sad little story: the mummified remains of a dockland cat with its claws still buried in the mummified body of a rat. Both had been found wedged beneath a warehouse during demolition.

Progress can be as ruthless as most corporate judgments, and containers have swept most of these sights and smells away from dockland. I wonder if the more sophisticated eyes and noses of those who strip the containers enjoy the same sensations of drama.

Royal, Surrey Commercial and Tilbury Docks

13

A T ROTHERHITHE, on the south bank, are the Surrey Commercial Docks, at the time of writing awaiting development. Their atmosphere was in complete contrast to the other, more urban, docks groups. Here was the result of piecemeal building by competing developers, followed by enforced amalgamations. The eleven interconnected dock basins had water areas ranging from some twenty-four acres to as little as two, and names which were pleasantly evocative of traditional trades. They were also connected with the Grand Surrey Canal, whose four miles were all that had materialized from the scheme to connect the Thames with Portsmouth.

The Greenland Dock in this group was on the site of the former Howland Great Wet Dock, London's first enclosed dock, used for the outfitting of ships. Greenland Dock took its name from London's former whaling industry, once centred there. Pieces of whalebone found on the site were imaginatively displayed in the outer walls of the post-war warehouse built on the site. It is said that Bishop Heber, the author of the hymn that begins "From Greenland's icy mountains to India's coral strand" was inspired by the sight of a ship outward bound for the Far East leaving this Greenland Dock.

Before they were blitzed, warehouses here dealt with Canadian dairy produce, but the main trade of this tangle of dock basins and storage ponds was imported softwood timber. North American spruce and pine were handled, but the bulk of the timber dealt with here came from the Baltic. Before the last European war, Surrey Docks were regularly invaded by a summer fleet of mixed ships under charter. Spindle-funnelled rust-streaked sea gypsies arrived with huge deck cargoes of deals, battens, scantlings and boards. Part of the fleet consisted of superannuated sailing vessels, some of them former beautiful fliers, now on their last sea legs. They were usually loaded with firewood—not wood for burning, but short ends of deals, battens and boards for the building trades. Many of these ships were so old that they were only kept afloat by windmill pumps revolving endlessly on their decks. These pumps groaned "onk-ur, onk-ur" and this gave the ships the

Opposite page:
Constructing the St Katharine Dock at Wapping, opened in 1828. From a contemporary print. Photo: Port of London Authority

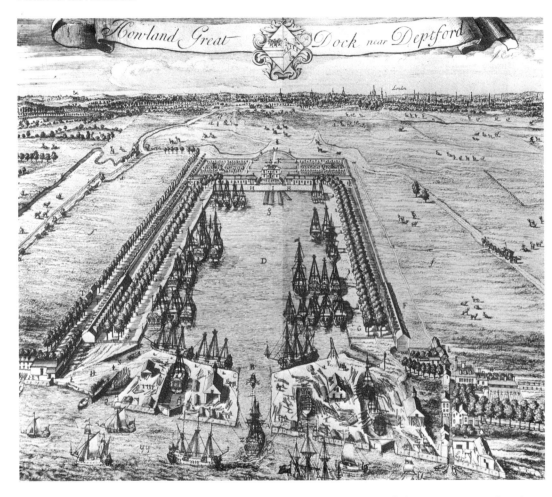

The Howland Great Wet Dock, built in the eighteenth century, was London's first enclosed wet dock. It became the basis of the Greenland Dock, part of the Surrey Commercial Docks at Rotherhithe.

London River name of onkurs. Many of the steamers and onkurs were loaded at dried-out berths and arrived in the Thames with frightening lists, only seaworthy because of their buoyant loads.

The timber was handled at the docks by deal porters, clannish men who worked in tightly knit gangs. The cargoes were piled to marks and numbers according to the importers' instructions, and the porters' skill was handed down from father to son. It consisted of weight lifting and balancing. The piles rose up forty or fifty feet, and the porters strode (often ran, for they were all on piece work) up a single-plank staging, balancing perhaps a complete fir scaffold pole or a number of planks, some twenty feet long, across their shoulders and the base of their necks. The load, often not far short of a hundredweight, caused a large callous, despite the protective leather backing, and this became the sign of their calling. Synchronizing the spring of the staging under their feet with the spring of the load on their shoulders, the deal porters were virtual acrobats. As the piles rose, small billets would be placed between each layer for ventilation.

Most of the narrow alleyways between the piles were carpeted with sawdust and bark and, when the deal porter had moved on, they were as silent as the forests of origin. Fugitive chinks of light turned the gloomy passages into veritable cathedral aisles, with incense from the resinous smell of the wood. Some of the large baulks and logs were kept stapled into rafts in the storage ponds. They were all clearly identified, and dockers who walked so surefootedly across the dipping, floating timber practised many of the skills of North American lumbermen.

Clean, quiet and fragrant, the Surrey Docks had wildlife denied the other upper docks. They cherished the lovely butterfly, Camberwell Beauty, and in the storage ponds were many small fish and several species of water birds—wild duck, swans, gannets, moorhens, seagulls and an occasional heron. Like the swans in the river, the ducks had an excellent intelligence service that told them which stacks of timber would not be soon disturbed by deliveries and under which it was therefore safe to nest.

In 1940 enemy aircraft made a dead set against these docks. During the London blitz, they were deluged with high explosive and incendiary bombs until some 250 acres of stacked timber became an inferno. Hundreds of firemen from as far away as Bristol and Rugby fought what was probably the biggest industrial fire in history*.

After the war, the PLA built what visiting Canadian lumbermen described as the world's finest timber storage sheds. With them marched new types of cranes and other equipment to alleviate the lot of the timber porters. Almost overnight, sheds, cranes and improved methods were rendered obsolete by the introduction of packaged timber—timber strapped together by steel bands and, in effect, a single unit—at the new Tilbury container port.

Before they were closed for redevelopment, the Royal Docks in the borough of Newham, the Royal Victoria, Royal Albert and King George V Docks, were the show piece of the port. All interconnected, they had a total water area of some 250 acres; they constituted, it was claimed, the world's largest sheet of impounded water. They handled the cream of the country's oversea trade and their shipping lines served every part of the world, either direct or

*The Thames on Fire by L. M. Bates (Terence Dalton, Ltd)

by transshipment. On a busy day, when up to fifty ships might have been berthed at the quays, there would be a double line, over three miles long, of ocean-going vessels. The principal entrance lock, King George V Lock, is 800 feet long and 100 feet wide, and on 6th August, 1939, I saw the new Cunarder *Mauretania*, the largest vessel to berth in these docks, pass through the entrance lock with little more than inches to spare.

Meat was a major theme at these docks. On the north side of the Royal Victoria Dock, huge consignments of chilled South American beef were discharged for transport to the meat markets. At the Royal Albert Dock, New Zealand lamb and mutton went into cold airstores where more than 300,000 carcases were normally held.

In the tobacco warehouses, huge cathedral-like shells, there was a suggestion of the mills of God in the working of the massive roof gantry cranes, which slowly travelled to and fro stowing the half-ton hogsheads of Virginia leaf. In other warehouses, tobacco in leaves of varied shape and size and each with its distinctive aroma and special blending qualities came from Africa, Greece, Turkey, China, Sumatra, Borneo, Japan, Korea, India and the West Indies and even from Ireland. PLA staff, acting on instructions from the importers, would draw representative samples of a consignment, and tobacco worth thousands of pounds would be bought unseen on the strength of their samples.

The south side of the Royal Victoria Dock was devoted to grain in bulk. Like the Millwall Dock, the privately owned flour mills sometimes berthed windships at the end of the so-called Australian grain race. This area had been devastated when a nearby munitions works at Silvertown blew up in 1917, killing sixty-nine people and injuring some four hundred. Grain discharge in this area was by suction elevator, but the men who manipulated the elevator pipes could remember when grain in bulk was discharged by basket and shovel. They were still known as toe-rags from the strips of cloth with which they kept the grain out of their boots.

Much general cargo arrived at these docks from the Far East. After the war, large consignments of raw rubber came from Malaya. The bales had been confiscated and stockpiled by the invading Japanese, and in the course of time many of the rubber sheets had fused. In some cases, the metal retaining bands had disappeared into shapeless lumps of rubber. To avoid damage to the manufacturers' machinery, PLA staff used wartime mine detectors to find the metal.

A special feature of the Royal Victoria Dock was the Exchange Rail Sidings, then said to be the largest in Europe. This vast network connected the Royal Docks with the country's main lines. Protection of cargo waiting overnight in rail trucks was a headache

for the dock police. On one occasion thieves had drilled through the floor of a locked truck and on into casks of liquor, which were drained into containers beneath the truck.

The Royal Victoria Dock (built in 1855) was the oldest of this group, and modernization of ramshackle quays, badly designed transit sheds and outdated equipment inherited from the former private dock company was only completed just in time to be overtaken by the container revolution which closed this group. Before the war, shabby old dock offices with breast-high desks, cold and badly lit, would have made worthy settings for the pen of Charles Lamb. Accountancy was still rooted in the previous century, and ledgers recording the arrival and departure of cargo were larger and heavier than paving stones. The covers of some bore telltale rings where nineteenth-century clerks had rested their beer mugs. Progress is a strange plant, for out of all this ancientry grew the modern port at Tilbury which keeps abreast, in some cases one jump ahead, of modern thinking and the latest technology.

Shipping in the Royal Docks at North Woolwich. These docks, formerly the pride of the Port, were the last of London's docks to be closed for development.
Photo: Stanley

157

Lords of these dock domains were HM Customs, who controlled the bonded warehouses and to whom every ounce of imported cargo had to be reported. When what was believed to be the first case of imported Mah Jong sets arrived at the Royal Victoria Dock, the terse bill of lading description "Chinese game" caused it to be entered for Customs' purposes under the heading "Poultry and Game" and sent to the Cold Store.

Helping to record this flow of cargo were the tally clerks. They would put a vertical stroke on their recording pad for every package that passed them, drawing diagonal lines through every file of four—the sign of the gate. This had evolved from the days when man first learnt to count on the fingers and thumb of one hand.

The Royal Albert Dock extends eastward from and is connected to the Royal Victoria Dock. Apart from a cold air store, it had no warehouses but was lined with transit sheds. In this accommodation, cargo was sorted to merchants' marks and numbers for delivery, and exports were collected into port consignments for loading. They were an essential part of oversea commerce.

A humble but valuable part in the export trade was played by the port colour marker. To help in the discharge of the ship in foreign ports where illiterate labour might have to be employed, the port marker daubed appropriate splashes of colour on the packages before loading. Thus all parcels marked with a certain colour would be for, say, Colombo, while another colour would be for Bombay, and so on.

The King George V Dock, opened in 1921 and then the most modern dock in the port, was linked in parallel to the Royal Albert Dock. Tobacco warehouses on the north side boasted the very latest form of underslung crane for handling the huge tobacco hogsheads. They could perform five different operations—hoisting, slewing, traversing, travelling and derricking. But these features did not save them from dockland development. Warehouses and cranes were swept away, and where the cranes reached and swung with their loads aircraft now take off and land at London's latest airport.

There were several reasons for the decline and eventual closure of this magnificent dock group. First was the decline in the warehousing trade which was London's most important contribution to oversea commerce. In the old days of long and uncertain ship passages and poor communication, merchants of this country had been glad to keep large stocks in bonded deck warehouses. After the war an importer could telephone for an appointment at the other side of the world, be there in a few hours and buy fresh supplies on the spot. And faster and more reliable ships meant that he need no longer keep capital tied up in warehoused goods. Despite dredging, there was a limit to the depths attainable in the river, and the ever larger ships could no longer navigate so far up river. Lastly, the new container trade demanded berths with some twelve to twenty acres of hinterland, and Tilbury alone among the docks of London had the undeveloped land necessary.

London is still this country's largest port and its trade is now encapsulated in this new container port at Tilbury in Essex. Twenty-five miles downstream of London Bridge, they were opened in 1886 by the East and West India Docks Company in the misguided hope of attracting trade before it ascended to the upper reaches. Before the war, Tilbury Docks were a somewhat neglected never-never land. With poor road communications, they relied on barge or rail links for cargo distribution. A feature of these docks before the war was the extent and variety of wildlife, not surpassed even by the Surrey Docks. Fired by what was premature optimism, the dock company had left the dock basins surrounded by hundreds of acres of land for future development. This area, today the site of container berths, was clothed in a summer jungle of cow

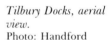

Tilbury Docks, aerial view.
Photo: Handford

parsley. Here and there were strange and sometimes exotic plants, probably brought there in cargo from far places.

Among the cow parsley were rabbits, stoats, an occasional fox, partridges, pheasants, hedgehogs and sparrow hawks. There was also an abundance of adders which sometimes nested under goods in the transit sheds. Farouche cats, civilized enough to respond to the noon whistle, used to emerge from the jungle to cadge titbits from the offices. Swans, ducks and several species of waterfowl swam in the basins. Asian seamen sometimes picked bundles of a sort of wild spinach growing in the area, and would go shrimping round the edges of the basins.

Before the war the PLA made considerable improvements at Tilbury Docks. A new entrance lock, 1,000 feet long and 110 feet wide, and a new dry dock, both still the largest in the port, were opened in 1929 and have since proved a basis for the more revolutionary changes of the nineteen-sixties. The dry dock has features then unique in ship repair; a leading-in girder grips the ship by its nose and ensures its position in the dock. When it comes to rest, automatic bilge blocks cradle the vessel, holding it upright in place of the former wooden supporting shores.

Most important of the changes here was the construction of the Tilbury Passenger Landing Stage, a riverside floating structure 1,142 feet long where the largest liners then using the port could remain afloat at all stages of the tide. It was opened in 1930 by J. Ramsay MacDonald, then Prime Minister. In those days, before the common man became blasé about travel, the departure of a ship from the Stage, the farewells, the promise of hotter suns and bluer seas, became a poignant affair.

On our journey down river we looked at the short ferry between Tilbury and Gravesend. In former days the long ferry between Tilbury and London Bridge was a much more comfortable way of travel than the highwayman-infested, unkempt roads.

The Stage was the setting for holiday cruises, which began before the war and are now being revived. The Stage was also a centre for the mass migration to the then Dominions and Colonies which began soon after the war. There were those, anxious about our home labour shortage, who claimed that the transfer of so many artisans and professional workers to overseas countries was merely robbing an impoverished Peter to pay a well-to-do Paul. Some claimed that the best were going, leaving the dregs behind, while others asserted that those who deserted their country in its post-war difficulties were not worth keeping.

At the time, I felt that the outlook of the emigrant himself might not be without some weight in the arguments. Accordingly, I joined at St Pancras Station one of the three special boat trains carrying between them a total of about nine hundred emigrants bound for Australia in the P&O liner *Ranchi* (broken up in 1953), awaiting them at the Tilbury Ocean Stage. This ship was one of a number on continuous charter to the Australian Government and had been converted into a one-class emigrant ship.

When I reached the station the train was already in. Practically all the passengers were out on the platform talking to relatives and friends; none of the migrants seemed so poor in human relationships as to have no one to see him off. Three things about the travellers struck me: their youthfulness, contrasting so strongly with the mainly middle-aged and elderly folk there to speed them; their children, for most of the separate parties appeared to include two or more youngsters; and their shining leather bags, unsophisticated in their innocent freedom from old labels.

The emigrants were all soberly dressed, and the going away atmosphere of a holiday train was markedly absent. One man, indeed, wore a bowler hat. The children, too, were apparently clad for the English rather than the Australian climate, and collectively would have provided an admirable background for a winter knitwear poster.

As the hands of the station clock jerked towards the departure hour, the passengers began to fidget and collect their scattered young. Voices became a little shrill and there was the same sort of air, part gaiety, part tension, that was found in camps and ships on the eve of D-Day. At last, with only two or three minutes to go, pretence was dispensed with; arms were flung round necks and much pent-up emotion spilled out to provide what must have been one of the most poignant mass scenes in peacetime London. Then it was "all aboard", and a hundred handkerchiefs and hands waved from train and platforms as we began to pull out. Old faces, puckered and creased with grief, slid past my window and then we were away.

I strolled through the vestibule of the train trying to marshal my impressions. Those migrants who had given way to emotion at the parting soon dried their eyes, for it is mainly those left behind who bear the burden of loss; those who depart have new scenes and different routines to divert their minds from grief. Nevertheless, I admired the fortitude of mothers who patted their children's hair into place and settled themselves resignedly in their seats. But I felt that the party of four who gave their children sweets to keep them quiet and began a game of cards were taking their exit from the homeland a little too lightly.

As opportunity offered, I spoke to some of the men. At least two of them were complete escapists who were leaving a land of February gloom and rain, high taxation, housing and food shortages, frustration and other features of a welfare state seemingly aiming at complete equality of misery, for a country where, they assured me, the sun always shone, where nothing was in short supply, and where much money was offered for little work. I made no attempt to disillusion them and left them hugging their unreal future.

More thoughtful was the ex-docker who admitted that he knew little about Australia and who recognized that life out there would present him with a lot of problems. He added: "But they'll be fresh problems; I'm tired of the old problems which I've had for so long in this country." Those I rather envied were the true adventurers. They were happy at making a change, careless of the future, unencumbered by many possessions and were prepared to make the best of whatever they found in the new land.

As I listened to the chatter along the coach I identified almost every accent in the British Isles. The tacky vowels of Yorkshire contrasted with the Gracie Fieldisms of the Lancastrian; the eroded syllables of the Cockney, the lyrical cadences of the Welshman, the well-padded tones of the West Countryman, the vibrating r's of the Scot, and the honey in the tones of the Irishman, pictured for me the scale of this migration.

Then I sat down and watched the war-battered London slums and grey suburbs, with their running gutters and spreading puddles, and tried to weigh up the reasons which some of these people had advanced for their departure. But on the whole, their motives were too mixed and amorphous to enable any particular feature to be pinpointed. I felt, however, that they all had one thing in common—their courage. The more urbanized and superficially secure our lives become, the more difficult it is to be courageous. These folk were not being driven out merely by hard times, for in that case the whole post-war nation would have been on the move. Rather, it seemed to me, they were expressing their refusal to accept hard times; in them was the instinct to fight against fate.

This led me to speculate that in the long run our loss might be a gain for what was then the Empire, and that the sorrow of some old grandmother left to her meagre meat ration in Balham or Doncaster would perhaps be compensated years thence by the rise of another Churchill or Smuts to save our older, increasingly decadent civilization, to whom the chance to serve might never have come but for the courage of his forbear in this emigrant train. For in courage are invariably found the seeds of leadership.

Nevertheless, as I again walked through the train, I decided that the little man by himself who played softly but discordantly on a mouth organ had obviously been forced to leave because he had made himself a nuisance. At first, I looked with rather superior tolerance at the steady munchings and drinkings going on; and I smiled to myself as I thought of the traditional shipboard fare awaiting them, rather like an outsize bone ready for a starved dog. But then I heard one young mother tell her neighbour that this was her little family's first chance to eat since they had left North Wales the previous night. This same family was utterly ignorant of ships and oceans, for as we passed a big reservoir, a piping treble asked: "Is that the sea, Mummy?" And the answer was inconclusive. As we neared Tilbury the clouds laddered and split, but the bare, drenched clay of the Essex fields rejected the advances of the watery sun, and I mentally contrasted their forlorn sullenness with the white beaches, flashing surf and vivid colours of the southern continent, and I marked another point to the credit of the passengers.

As we ran into the Riverside Station there was much stir in the coaches, and the smell of new leather became overpowering (no plastics in those days!) as bags were hauled off luggage racks and piled in readiness for detraining. But as the train stopped, a loud-speaker told everyone to keep to their seats. For some fifteen minutes the passengers chattered and fidgeted while their baggage was taken to the Baggage Hall by a fleet of electric trucks and there sorted to names and piled under the great letters pendant from the roof. Then the emigrants were formed into a long crocodile in the station circulating hall. It was then that "Port Welfare (1946) Tilbury" appeared, and six or seven nursing sisters of that voluntary organization helped mothers overburdened with young children. In some cases, babies were taken over by the nurses, leaving the parents to deal with bags and formalities.

The routine was simple and surprisingly quick. The long line of passengers first passed a desk, where they rid themselves of money in excess of the amount then permitted to be taken out of the country. Arrangements existed whereby the P&O sent a draft for the excess to await the passengers' arrival in Australia. Then the crocodile writhed back on itself to pass through the Immigration Office, where passports were stamped and the last link with austerity, the ration book, was surrendered. After that the crocodile dissolved, and waiting porters led the passengers to the piles of baggage. This was wheeled up to the counter of HM Customs, who satisfied themselves that the bags contained no prohibited exports. Finally the bags were wheeled down the brow to the landing stage, where waiting ranks of Goanese stewards took the baggage and led the owners to their cabins.

On board, everything was ready for their reception: comfortable bunks, linen, hot water and other features of the ship's vast passenger organization were at their disposal. In family parties the emigrants flocked into the saloon, where an excellent meal awaited them. Some of the more humble passengers, particularly the little man with the mouth organ, were obviously awed by the surroundings. There seemed, indeed, little difference between the napery, table furnishings, menu and service provided and those in a first-class liner. Looking round the saloon, I thought of Charles Dickens's description of the departure of emigrants from Gravesend in his day:

> Among the great beams, bulks and ringbolts of the ship, and the emigrant berths and chests, and bundles and barrels, and heaps of miscellaneous baggage . . . lighted up, here and there, by dangling lanterns, and elsewhere by the yellow daylight straying down a windsail or hatchway . . . were crowded groups of people . . . some already settled down into the possession of their few feet of space, with their little household arranged . . .

Times had, indeed, changed, and have changed even more drastically for migrants now departing from Heathrow or Gatwick. At last all was ready and the great ship moved off; all the emotion seemed to have been spilled at St Pancras, and none of the emigrants at the vessel's rail displayed any signs of regret at leaving.

Watching the ship draw away from the landing stage, I found a distinguished merchant seaman of my acquaintance. Knowing of his long connection with Australia, I told him that I felt these emigrants were both wise and courageous in their decision to seek new opportunities. He snorted. "If", he said, "they were going to farm or take up real pioneering, I couldn't agree with you more. But ninety-nine per cent will merely change into an identical environment, eleven thousand miles away. The typist, sick of typing in a London office, will type in a similar office in another city; the plumber, tired of losing his tools and his mate, will lose similar tools and mate overseas."

I felt that he was prejudiced and that whatever he said these emigrants had at least shown courage and initiative in uprooting themselves. But as the last rays of the sun turned the uncertain waters of Gravesend Reach into sequins and silk, and the flapping topsail of a spritsail barge into hammered gold, the Thames looked good—possibly as good as the Murrumbidgee or the Murray River. And with that thought in my mind, I realized that that was where I had come in and that I had made no real progress in settling the tideway arguments.

Tilbury Docks produced a record of an earlier migration, of immigrants who followed Roman forces. When the dry dock was excavated, a stone tablet bearing a Greek inscription commemorating the wife of a Greek citizen of Roman Londinium was found. Archaeologists suggested that it had probably been carried down river in one of the loads of soil removed during the construction of London's first underground railway and dumped on the Essex marsh before the docks were built.

The Port of London 14
Authority

I DON'T think anyone would have dared to label the first Lord
Devonport "Docker" but in effect he was the founder of the
modern Port of London. Near the end of the last century,
London's overseas commerce was being very badly served by
outdated docks under their various private owners while the tidal
river, administered by the Thames Conservancy Board, was unable
to accommodate the larger ships coming into service.

A Royal Commission resulted in the Port of London Authority
being created in 1908 to take over the enclosed docks and
conservancy of the tidal river. Its first chairman was Sir Hudson
Kearley, later Lord Devonport. He was an organizing genius
driven by an autocratic impatience which made him feared by his
underlings. The arrival of this frock-coated figure at the PLA
offices or at the docks kept everyone on his toes. Under the
whiplash of his tongue, a huge dredging programme deepened the
river, the quite-new King George V Dock was built, plans to
modernize the other docks were laid, and the palatial former
offices of the PLA on Tower Hill in the City were erected. This
building, full of the adornments and curlyqueues beloved of the
Victorians, was described by an irreverent architectural journal as
"Directors' Grecian".

During a visit to a dock warehouse, he decided to buy some
carpets stored there. The owner, an Armenian Jew, was sum-
moned to the chairman's private office. Presently Devonport's
angry voice and the banging of a desk were heard by fascinated
listeners in the outer office. When the owner of the carpets finally
emerged, pale and shaken, he was asked if the chairman had in fact
bought the carpets. "Yes", was his reply. "But I don't know whether
he is to give me a cheque or if I am to give him one."

In 1911 the dockers asked for a revision of pay and conditions,
which had not altered since 1889. Impatient to press on with his
plans, Devonport, together with other port employers, granted pay
increases totalling £200,000 a year and other concessions. To the
men, it was a case of too little, too late, and a dock strike began.
Public opinion was, on the whole, behind the dockers, but
Devonport was unmoved. "I will starve them into submission", he
coldly announced.

Towards the end of the strike, the men's bitterness led them to

Viscount Davenport, PC, the aggressive first chairman of the Port of London Authority. Portrait by Z. Nemethy after de Lásló.
Photo: Port of London Authority

a meeting on Tower Hill, where one of their leaders, Ben Tillett, asked them to kneel and join him in prayer. "Oh, God," they intoned, "please strike the PLA chairman dead." Their prayer was unanswered. After ten weeks of chaos in the port, the strike collapsed and the work of development was resumed.

Devonport retired in 1925 and died in 1934. He left behind industrial unrest which created the strong spirit of unity among dockers, but, at the same time, he left a port which claimed to be the world's greatest.

Lord Devonport was succeeded as PLA chairman by Lord Ritchie of Dundee, whose family backcloth was imported jute. He was a man of mixed character. On the one hand he was a gifted amateur sculptor who once claimed that every artist, ceaselessly seeking unattainable perfection, needed a companion to hit him over the head when enough was enough. On the otherhand, when an embryo publicity department submitted its first effort, an aerial view of the port and its docks with the caption "London, the world's greatest port", he turned it down with the remark: "It savours of vulgar boasting."

In an earlier writing* I described an incident as happening to the master of an excursion steamer; I had substituted the seaman for Lord Ritchie as a matter of discretion. The true story is as follows. Lord Ritchie issued an annual invitation to Westminster School, where he had been educated, to a cruise through dockland in the PLA steam yacht *St Katharine*. The event took place one autumn when the press was full of seasonal pictures of East End families off for their annual holiday, hop picking in Kent. The *St Katharine* passed rather close to a lighterman tugging at the huge oars of his craft and he paused to look up at Lord Ritchie, surrounded by schoolboys wearing the traditional toppers and tail coats. "Where you going with that lot, mate?" he asked. " 'Opping?" His Lordship was not amused and I was in disgrace for laughing.

After Munich, plans were made for a local wartime Emergency Committee, representing all its varied interests (virtually the Port of London Authority but enlarged and with much wider powers) to take over if war came and ensure the continuity of the port's essential operations. When hostilities began, the PLA under the chairmanship of Lord Ritchie until his early retirement and then under the Rt Hon. Thomas Wiles, PC, continued to function in a muted role as well as being part of the Emergency Committee. The Navy moved into the PLA head offices to assume responsibility for the defence and naval administration of the port. Thomas Wiles

The Londoner's River by L. M. Bates (Muller, 1949).

successfully co-operated in dealing with often-conflicting problems while keeping the civilian administration functioning under a prolonged hail of bombs and incendiaries.

When Thomas Wiles retired soon after the end of the war, he was succeeded as PLA chairman by Sir John Anderson, later Lord Waverley. His long career in public service—Minister of Home Security, Lord President of the Council and Chancellor of the Exchequer—brought exceptional qualities to the port's administration.

The Rt Hon. Lord Ritchie of Dundee, Chairman of the PLA from 1925 to 1941. From the painting by Francis Dodd, RA. Photo: Port of London Authority

Those of us who worked with him knew that he would have achieved distinction in almost any career or profession. While fishing in Wales many years ago, I met a charming Scots lady whose brother had been a contemporary of Anderson at George Watson's School. She told me that even as an immature schoolboy his fellows foresaw a great future for him. In later life, one of his tenets, that sloppy speech and slovenly thinking go together, was reflected in his own erudite, perhaps rather pedantic, expressions. But his meaning was always clear, and he was that rare leader who makes a success of rule by committee.

The chief attribute of the long line of merchant venturers and seamen who developed the Port of London has been courage. On that score, Anderson was fully worthy of those traditions. Throughout his public career he was almost invariably selected for the most difficult Governmental posts—shipping during the First World War, Ireland during the beginning of the troubles, Bengal in the days of the terrorists, civil defence on the eve of the Second World War, etc—posts which required not only administrative genius but considerable moral and physical courage. After the dastardly attempt to assassinate him at the Lebong Race Course at Darjeeling in 1934, a colleague rushed round to Government House to express his relief at Sir John's escape. He was greeted with: "Never mind about that. You're just in time to play me 250 up." If he had a reputation for sternness, it arose from his refusal to compromise with assassins or trifle with anarchy and murder. That his sternness was tempered by mercy was evidenced by his treatment of the Bengali youth who attempted the assassination. He was sentenced to death by a Court of Justice, but Sir John, as Governor, commuted the sentence to one of life imprisonment. Assured that the youth had relinquished his belief in violence, he pardoned him and facilitated his passage to an English university.

It was said of Sir John Anderson that with the possible exception of Mr Winston Churchill no other man had held so many distinguished appointments. His most brilliant success was probably his six years' tenure of the Governorship of Bengal. He went there in the country's time of need, for terrorism was active, famine

167

The Rt Hon. Viscount Waverley of Westdean, PG, GGM, OM, GCSI, FRS. From the painting by Harold Knight. Waverley was Chairman of the PLA from 1946 to 1958.
Photo: Port of London Authority

threatened, trade and finance tottered, and general revolution crouched in the immediate future. He was greeted coldly by a hostile Press, who interpreted his reputation for discipline and justice as repressive and tyrannical. When he left Bengal at the end of his term of office, it was amidst genuine and almost unanimous regret, and even his earlier critics expressed their conviction that he had saved Bengal from anarchy. His mark was left on the country's agriculture, trade, finance and administration. During his governorship, he not infrequently went on informal walking tours from Darjeeling into Sikkim or Tibet, often accompanied by the Indian Civil Service officer who knew most about the flora of the Himalayas. What better way of studying the problems of a country so largely dependent upon its agriculture and natural resources?

Mr Harold Nicolson wrote in *The Spectator*, apropos Sir John Anderson: "Although an extremely modest man, (he) is able without effort to impart information regarding the incidence of the land tax in the Punjab, the location of tourmalines and the functions of the olfactory organs in cyclostomes." Turning back the pages of Sir John Anderson's career, one finds some explanation of this omniscience in a unique breadth of experience: secretary to the Northern Nigerian Lands Committee, secretary to the West African Currency Committee, secretary to the Insurance Commissioners, additional secretary to the Local Government Board, second secretary to the Ministry of Health, chairman of the Board of Inland Revenue, under-secretary to the Lord Lieutenant of Ireland, etc. But after Bengal, it was probably in shipping that he made his most useful contribution to his country's welfare. During his speech to the cadets in HMS *Worcester* at an annual distribution of prizes, he revealed his pride in a forebear who had been a master mariner; perhaps this explains to some extent his invaluable work as secretary to the Ministry of Shipping during the dark days of 1917 to 1919, for his grasp of wartime shipping problems needed something more than administrative genius to explain. Among other measures, he was largely responsible, in the face of the misgivings of the Royal and Merchant Navies, for instituting the convoy system which then, as during the Second World War, alone sustained the country's oversea life-line.

Among Sir John's many interests, the subject of science was very near his heart. The famous Anderson shelter was no lucky solution of a great national problem; it was the result of a deep personal interest and scientific study of the effects of total war upon a civilian population. Formerly chairman of the Advisory Committee on Atomic Energy, he had a profound belief in the ability of applied science to solve many of our national problems. In a number of speeches he had stressed the need to make full use of our scientific discoveries in the industrial field, and he held the view that science must become part of the background of the country's administrators. He was the instigator of and took a great interest in the scientific inquiries which brought the Thames back to life.

After the war, the foaming beer-coloured liquid that sluiced past the piers and barge roads not only stank as never before but was also rejecting attempts to increase and in some cases even to maintain the depth of the dredged channel. It was known that pollution and siltation were linked and were largely due to the same causes: the over-burden of sewage effluent (500 million gallons daily), mostly only partly treated, which robbed the water of oxygen and caused it to drop its load of silt instead of carrying it to sea; the dumping of industrial waste; the amount of fresh water taken from the non-tidal river for London's taps; and the raising of river temperatures by the discharge of large volumes of hot water from the growing number of riverside electricity generating stations.

Backed by his considerable scientific education (Edinburgh and Leipzig universities) Sir John set up a special committee and brought in the Government Department of Scientific and Industrial Research. A full investigation of pollution and siltation began. In the course of the inquiry, minute quantities of radioactive mud were launched in order to trace the movement of silt.

A large working model of the river bed, four hundred feet long, and its tides (generated electronically) complete with model silt was built in a shed at the Royal Victoria Dock. To watch the tide ebbing and flowing through the model's channel was fascinating. The full twelve and a half hour tide cycle was condensed to thirteen and a half minutes. When my ship was running out of Sheerness during the war, we had sometimes encountered a powerful eddy at certain states of the tide where the waters of the Medway met those of the Thames. I saw this eddy faithfully reproduced in miniature on the model. In the meantime, Sir John was bringing his formidable oral artillery to bear on the LCC (later GLC) regarding the further treatment of sewage; on the Central Electricity Generating Board and its riverward discharge of hot water, and on Thames-side industry to stop using the river as a dustbin.

In 1957 the committee's report (backed by a later report on effluent by a Government committee under Professor A. J. S. Pippard) resulted in several important measures. The LCC pressed on with improvements already in hand at their sewage outfalls at Beckton and Crossness in the middle tideway and polluting discharges were put out of bounds. Then the PLA ceased its traditional method of dumping silt brought up by its dredgers: silt which the inquiry proved soon returned to the fairway from the

The working tidal model of the Thames, built in the search for a healthier river, covered most of the floor of a transit shed at the Royal Victoria Dock.
Photo: Hydraulics Research Station

dumping ground in the Black Deep in the outer estuary. Henceforth it was pumped ashore for marsh reclamation.

In less than a decade the results were surprising. Costly maintenance dredging was reduced and the depths of ship channels improved. Wildfowl returned to the river in ever greater numbers, and where hardly any fish had formerly existed a great variety, including the finicky rainbow trout, began to appear on the suction grids of riverside power stations.

On 1st April, 1974, statutory control of river purification along the tideway passed from the PLA to the Thames Water Authority. Still later, the National Rivers Authority was created to co-operate with Thames Water. Aided by the most scientific equipment, it has carried on where the PLA left off, and the tidal Thames is now one of the world's healthiest and cleanest industrial rivers.

A problem that persists comes from the London sewage system, built in the last century. It is unable to cope with severe storm surges. This may deprive certain river reaches of oxygen and cause the death of fish. To overcome this, oxygen is pumped into the afflicted reaches by the *Thames Bubbler*, a vessel specially designed and equipped for this operation.

In the Civil Service, because of his omniscient pronouncements, Sir John was known as Jehovah. And there was, indeed, something almost godlike in his conduct of PLA affairs. But occasionally the mask would crack. Presiding at a staff social function, he awaited the arrival of Lady Waverley (his second wife). She was not noted for being punctual and his irritation visibly increased as she failed to appear on time to perform some opening ceremony. When at last she arrived, he called for order with such vehemence that he broke his gavel. He gave his audience a charming smile. "Excess of zeal", he explained, "has caused me to break my gavel."

Sir John Anderson was created Viscount Waverley in 1952. In 1958 the much-prized Order of Merit was presented to him as he lay in hospital on what was to be his death bed. Full of well-deserved honours, he died that year, but nowhere is there a memorial to the man who first began to revive the dying Thames.

Lord Waverley was succeeded as PLA chairman by Viscount Simon of Stackpole Elidor, a former director of the P&O Steamship Company. For fifty years the Authority had been cutting out the dead wood and bringing new growth to the docks inherited from the moribund private companies. Economic crises and two world wars had slowed the programme, but under Lord Simon the work was at last completed. The Thames Navigation Service was introduced. New quays, new sheds and warehouses, and new equipment were now operated by new thinking. But the PLA did not have time for pleased contemplation of the revived port, for almost overnight the container revolution began to change sea carriage. The new sheds and warehouses were not needed, the new equipment was scrapped and the new thinking had to give place to yet newer thinking. The London, St Katharine, Surrey Commercial, East and West India, and Royal Docks were closed, one by one, and handed over to developers with little or no interest in ships and their cargoes. And the new style Port of London became encapsulated in the Tilbury Docks in Essex. Lord Simon, the most democratic of all PLA chairmen, was the link between the port's colourful past and its pragmatic present.

And there, so far as I was personally concerned with PLA chairmen, history, to quote Seller and Yeatman, came to an end.

Members of the PLA Board were either elected or appointed. Most were there to serve the interests they represented. One at least, Admiral Sir Alan Hotham, was also devoted to the port *qua* the country's largest sea terminal. He was an elderly bachelor, looked after by his former coxswain; he boasted that his overcoat, green with age, had belonged to his grandfather. On one occasion, after he had conducted a party of distinguished visitors round the port in the PLA yacht *St Katharine*, an American businessman who had been among the guests asked me who the old gentleman was who had explained the workings of ships and cargoes. When I told him that it had been Sir Alan Hotham, he gasped. "Gee!" he exclaimed. "I nearly gave him half a dollar."

The only other board member who impinged on me was Tom Scoulding. Elected Alderman and Mayor of West Ham Borough Council and appointed a Justice of the Peace, he represented Labour for the Ministry of Transport on the PLA Board. Several other honours came to him in old age. When he was apprenticed lighterman in 1892 he worked a seventy-two-hour week for eight shillings, and an all-night shift would bring a further one shilling and sixpence. When he was "out of his time" in 1898 he received the full wages for a lighterman: six shillings for a twelve-hour day spread over fourteen hours of attendance, with another four shillings for a short night up to midnight, and another two shillings if he worked a full night.

A passionate fighter for the then exploited port worker, Tom became a full-time trade union official in 1903. But before that his natural pugnacity had landed him in trouble with the police during a dock strike. When he appeared in the dock at Grays Police Court, the magistrate looked gloomily at him and then asked the Court to stand. "I have", the magistrate said, "a very sad and solemn announcement to make." Tom gasped. This must be the prelude to the black cap! "I have received news", the magistrate went on, "of the death of our gracious Sovereign, Queen Victoria. Long live the King." Tom was acquitted.

As a former Chancellor of the Exchequer, Lord Waverley's grasp of finance was on a very high plane. He was once holding forth to the PLA Board on port costs. Few of the members were mentally equipped to follow him. When he had finished, there was a dead silence while the audience marshalled its thoughts. Then Tom piped up. "Well, we've all got to 'elp one another, ain't we."

Pugnacious in youth, he was a peace maker in old age, and when he died he was mourned by a multitude of friends.

Administration of the PLA was based on Civil Service lines, but some Thames individualism rubbed off on its executives. The PLA General Manager under Lords Devonport and Ritchie was Sir David Owen. He did much to further the port's rebirth, but the strain sometimes affected his temper. Chairing a selection committee interviewing young assistant dockmasters applying for a vacant post as dockmaster, he was in a bad temper. As the young hopefuls came and went one by one, he was increasingly waspish and sarcastic about their qualifications. Until one young man lost his temper, too. "I didn't come here to be insulted by you, Sir David", he roared. And he departed, banging the door behind him for good measure. There was an ominous silence among the committee; no one had ever before been known to speak like that to Sir David. He, too, was silent for a moment. Then he said: "That's our man. I knew I'd get something out of one of them if I tried hard enough."

Sir David had two hobbies. The first was to establish the Welshness of the Port. He was convinced that ancient men of Wales had left the flint knives and arrow heads which the dredgers sometimes brought up. He was dejected when the coins thrown to appease the river gods at the former ford near London Bridge were found to be of Roman origin. But he brightened when many of the coins proved to be counterfeit, saved by thrifty early Londoners for the gods. And he did much research to prove that the name London was a corruption of a Celtic description of the "Place by the Pool".

His other hobby was reading pulp Westerns. He brought them as they came out, read them and then passed them on to PLA messenger boys. This distraction inspired him to write his own Western. His characters, who were quick on the draw in defeating dastardly outlaws, were thinly drawn from his PLA colleagues. *Colorado Jones* (the hero had, of course, to be Welsh) was published at his own expense and sank without trace.

The PLA general managers who followed Sir David were less eccentric. Sir Douglas Ritchie's work as Chief Executive of the Wartime Emergency Committee has already been recorded*. After him came Mr Theophilus Williams, a keen fly fisherman. He wrote to me just before his death saying that he hoped to find oblivion and escape a "Jew's paradise of harps and cherubim". "But", he added, "I shan't mind if I get a bit of fishing." Sir Leslie Ford presided over the "final" modernization of the port, and Mr Dudley Perkins ("Can I help you" of BBC broadcasts) introduced the new container port.

A few anecdotes will serve to show that Thames-side eccentricity and individualism rubbed off on minor PLA officials more strongly. One assistant manager had an unconscious gift for mixed metaphor. A then current exhortation, "Step on the gas!", became "Step on the gas pipe". He turned "Life is not a bed of roses" into "a bed of rose trees". And one could not have one's bread buttered on both sides of the bread "and in the middle as well".

My friend, John, acquired a new silk umbrella which became

his pride and joy. One morning, when he arrived at the office, he was clutching a seedy old gamp and was full of despair. "Took the wrong one off the luggage rack", he moaned. "I don't suppose . . ." he began and then stopped. And a huge smile spread over his face. "I've just remembered," he laughed. "I didn't bring my umbrella this morning."

For publicity purposes the PLA employed a firm of model makers. The Managing Director was as full of yarns as any old Thamesman. His best story was about himself leaving art school and getting his first commission, to provide a decorative border round a page of advertisements. The editor concerned had a reputation for beating down the price of such work, and my friend lay awake wondering whether to charge as much as thirty shillings for the job. When he handed in the copy, the editor banged his desk and roared: "How much?" The young man's courage failed and he replied weakly: "I thought . . . say . . . twenty-five . . ." Before he could say more, the editor roared: "Pounds, pounds, not guineas. You bloody artists always want guineas."

The closer to the tides, the more eccentricity emerged. One dockmaster, on leaving the Seven Seas Club, then at Charing Cross Pier, found landmarks had disappeared under a thick fog. He jumped into a waiting taxi, saying "Richmond". When the driver started going round back streets, he protested. "This isn't the way to Richmond", he said. "Fog's so thick, I'm going to pick up a mate to walk in front", replied the cabby. "Not necessary," said the dockmaster "I know the way"; and it is alleged that he walked in front of the taxi all the way to Richmond.

I realize now that I need not have differentiated between dockers and people of the river. They were all the same non-conformist breed, idiosyncratic, independent and cherishing a robust sense of humour. They reflected the tides and they helped the tides to make London what it is.

Looking back on these writings, the great freight of time past sinks on me. The quays, the warehouses, the fragrances and stinks have gone. All the men I mentioned by name, with the exception of three, are dead. Several of the round-bellied watermen's pubs, where Thames-side stories became lore, have either disappeared under development or degenerated into restaurants or gin palaces. Beautiful ships with attractive names have been supplanted by what look like floating football pitches, labelled to match. Riverside churches . . . But why go on? Old age cannot halt the great wheel of change. And, despite all the development, the Thames flows on.

The Thames on Fire by L. M. Bates (Terence Dalton, Ltd)

Tugs of London River   15

A WATCHER on the Gravesend waterfront, seeing a stream-lined tug spurning the tide into a white cascade as she hurries, nose disdainfully tilted, to meet some inbound ship, would never again describe such craft as fussy. They are elegant, powerful, purposeful, and their design is the result of more than a century of line breeding.

When sail still crowded the tidal Thames, vessels too large to tack in the comparatively narrow waterway either waited for a fair wind or were towed by ship's boats. It was not until the eighteen-thirties that the commercial steam tug appeared; she was built of wood, propelled by paddles driven by a primitive engine. Tugs were so small—only 20 to 30 tons—that coal bunkers were minute, and when the seven or eight tons of coal ran out at awkward moments they sometimes had to borrow fuel from the galley of the tow.

By the eighteen-fifties, these tugs had grown in size and had better bunkering capacity, but they were still built of wood and driven by paddle wheels. These larger craft began the romantic trade of "seeking"—setting out on spec. as far down Channel as Ushant in the hope of a profitable bargain over the rope of some heavily laden windship. Smaller tugs, known as toshers, were also being developed to compete with the traditional lighterman, who with his huge oars and profound local knowledge had hitherto had a monopoly of driving his big dumb barges with the tides.

Colonial clippers, berthed in the London and St. Katharine Docks, those situated further upstream and therefore with the longest stretch of river between them and the sea, began to advertise for passengers with the claim that the ships would "take steam" as far as Gravesend.

London tugmen today are among the most progressive of Thamesmen, but their forebears were some of the most conservative. The fight between screw and paddles was protracted on the high seas, but it took even longer to convince tug owners that paddles, however efficient in sudden calls to go astern, had been killed by the more powerful thrust and greater economy of the propeller. It took almost as long for wooden hulls to be supplanted by iron and then by steel.

The watermen in those old steam tugs, before their bridges

became festooned with modern electronic aids, were among the toughest and most self-reliant Thames-siders. The chief engineer, usually a shovel engineer ie, one who had graduated from the stokehold without a certificate, had an uncanny r'approchement with the captain. Often grumbling about the bridge being too fond of backing and filling (a term handed down from the days of sail), he would be ready at the throttle to give a touch ahead or astern almost before the engine-room telegraph had rung.

Lucrative salvage work looms large in the tug story, and we have already looked at hovels and what they meant to the crews. Radar and other modern navigational aids and radio communication, now focused on ships using the port by the Thames Navigation Service, have made the hovel a rarity.

During the two world wars, Thames tugs did valuable work in salvaging mined or torpedoed ships, but their greatest wartime contribution was undoubtedly during the Dunkirk lift. While the small lighterage tugs kept the port of London functioning, practically all the bigger towage tugs joined the miscellaneous collection of ships and craft that went to save the army. They dodged the shells and bombs, plucked big ships out of trouble and made several passages between Dunkirk and the Thames laden with soldiers.

Before the closure of the upper docks, there was much work for the tugs, escorting big ships up and down the tideway. For most of the passage, they merely accompanied the vessel, ready to take a line and give her a sheer if needed, or prevent her swinging if she had to anchor. Inward-bound ships would take a line from the tug off the dock entrance to help her straighten up. Then the tug or tugs would aid her into the lock. Much local knowledge was needed in this work, for the twenty-foot rise and fall of Thames tides creates a fast ebb or flow past the dock pier-head which the tug might have to counter.

Formerly, inside the enclosed docks and now only in Tilbury Docks, towage was carried out by PLA tugs. They would tow the ship to her berth and then, if necessary, the dock tug's bow pudding (the massive rope fendoff cloaking the stem) would be gently placed against the ship's side to give her a final nudge into her berth.

Opposite page: Challenge, *built in 1931, the last Thames steam tug in service, about to join a floating museum at St Katharine Dock in 1973. She was typical of the craft used in the Dunkirk evacuation.*

After the war, like most of the country, the Port of London and its tugs paused to get breath back. Many lessons learnt during hostilities had to be assimilated before the London towage trade took off once more. First came the introduction of the diesel engine, which tradition had resisted before the war, but which was now inevitable. In the first place, the reliability of the diesel engine had been proved by countless wartime ships and craft; also the engines could be started from scratch without the long wait to raise

steam. They allowed direct control from the bridge and were more economical in maintenance and manpower. Radar, VHF and other aids came in, and the Thames tugmaster began to evolve into something of a technologist, but one who still had to practise the skills and know the ancient tidal lore of the Thames waterman.

Today, the tugs of London River are large and powerful craft, their design suited to local conditions, although many of them are capable of long ocean tows. As is usual in tugs, they have their towing hook nearly amidships; this reduces the danger of getting girded, ie allowing the tow to take charge of the tug, which might then be in danger of capsizing. Most are equipped with powerful salvage pumps and other fire-fighting gear. Their crews average seven in number. The craft range in size up to about 115 feet and generate up to about 2,100 brake horse power. Compare this with the little wooden *Monarch*, one of Watkins's first tugs, which appeared in the Thames in 1833; she was only just over 64 feet and had an engine of 20 horse power.

With the closing of so many upriver docks, PLA dock tugs have declined from thirteen craft to four. These operate in Tilbury Docks. Well suited to confined waters, they are all diesel-engined and Voith-Schneider propelled. This involves an adjustable thrust propeller set flush in the bottom of the hull just forward of the bridge. It is used both to steer and propel and provides large steering power at low speeds. These tugs can turn through 360 degrees on their own axis, and can move sideways as well as ahead and astern. Somewhat less powerful than the river tugs, not being required to make long ocean tows and operating in non-tidal waters, they generate some 1,600 horse power. They are crewed by between five or six men.

The wind of change has blown no less strongly through the private tug companies than through the port generally. Famous old London towage companies such as Watkins, Dick and Page, W. H. J. Alexander and others have been merged into the Alexandra Towing Company (London) Ltd. It was Watkins's tug *Anglia* which in 1878 salvaged Cleopatra's Needle, broken adrift in the Bay of Biscay, and brought it safely to London. This craft was known as *Three Finger Jack* from the number and position of her funnels.

The days when tug owners walked round the City with a bag of sovereigns, collecting dues and paying debts, have given way to costing accountancy, work study and computers, all in keeping with the elegant and efficient tugs at the Gravesend buoys. However, like the tug masters, this sophistication only functions satisfactorily when backed by a basic knowledge of tides, ships and craft.

With the decline of the lighterage trade, not many lighterage tugs are left. However, those that remain have also evolved to meet modern situations. They are very robust and able to withstand

Sun Essex *is a typical vessel of the modern Sun fleet. She is equipped with all possible navigational aids and has powerful fire-fighting and salvage pumps. But just like the men in the old steam tugs, her crew must have a very wide knowledge of tidal lore.*

A splendid vessel, Sun *was built in 1906 and scrapped in 1964. She was one of the former Sun fleet of steam tugs.*

repeated contact with barges. They, too, have passed from steam to diesel. Their skippers have skills somewhat different from those of the ship-tug masters. With a standard tow of not more than six barges (a PLA River Bye-law) they and their long tails have to negotiate other traffic in an often crowded fairway, all moving with the tide. Barges, sometimes only a single one, may have to be manoeuvred by one of the attendant lightermen into or out of the flock, while the tug and the rest of the tow either slow down or stem the tide.

Tugs are ships in miniature and appeal to the small boy in most men. That father figure among our scientists, Thomas H. Huxley, once said he thought he would like to have been a tug if he had not been a man*.

*The Huxleys by R. W. Clark (Heinemann, 1968).

Cordillera Express, *a modern container ship fully laden, about to berth at the container terminal in Tilbury Docks.*
Photo: Port of London Authority

Ship Histories 16

BEFORE the middle nineteen-sixties, when the container began to undermine centuries of tradition, there were, on an average day, more than a hundred ships berthed in London's docks, with a score or more alongside private riverside wharves or moored in the stream. With their regular arrivals at the same berths, most of these vessels were seamarks, so that a reference to the Blue Star line or British India Steam instantly connoted Royal Docks, or, say, Ben Line, the West India group.

Some of the ships normally berthing in the river have been described; the cream of London's shipping was to be found at the docks. The stories behind many of these vessels constitute a microcosm of British history. The windships we met during our passage down river, which did so much to spread democracy and the British Commonwealth across the world, were often progenitors of modern liners.

Berthed in the London Docks there was usually a ship of General Steam Navigation, a company claiming to be the oldest ocean-going steamship company in the world, which we met at Irongate Wharf on our way downstream. Nearby berthed the "Coasts" of Coast Lines, which served more than a score of British ports. Scotland was linked to the Thames by Clyde Shipping vessels, all named after lighthouses, the Aberdeen Steam Navigation, the Dundee, Perth and London Line and London and Edinburgh Shipping. The last three usually used berths at riverside wharves.

Irish ports were visited by the British and Irish steam packets and the famous old City of Cork vessels. The City of Cork company owned the little *Sirius*, the first vessel to cross the Atlantic under continuous steam power; that was in 1838. In modern times, the company was content to stick to coasting.

A story about the City of Cork flag resembles the yarn we picked up at Blackwall about the Green and Wigram flag. The City of Cork line, like Green and Wigram, chose a St George's Cross for their house flag, and it, too, was ordered to be struck by the Navy as resembling an Admiral's flag. When the master refused, HMS *Dryad* sent away a boat's crew to impound it. The master seems to have handled the situation with even more determination than the officer in the *Sir Edward Paget*, for it is said that he literally nailed up his colours, greased the mast stays and successfully defied the Navy. But eventually the company had to give way, and the flag design was changed.

Downstream, at the West India Docks, we begin to meet larger vessels. The banana berth at these docks, where the fruit was dealt with automatically and counted by a selenium cell, was served by the Jamaica Direct Fruit Line. Like other imports we had taken for granted, bananas disappeared during the war. In 1946, the *Jamaica Producer*, the first banana ship to discharge in London when the ban on such imports was lifted, berthed in these docks, and the first stem of bananas to be landed was ceremoniously greeted by the Mayor of Poplar.

From the Chinese crews of the Ben Line which berthed in the West India Docks I picked up the wartime story of Poon Lim, second steward of the *Benlomond*, torpedoed in the South Atlantic with tragic loss of life. Poon Lim was washed into the sea but miraculously found a raft which carried water and food for some fifty days. He, however, managed to survive for no less than 133 days by catching fish on a hook which he fashioned from a nail drawn with his bare teeth from a plank, and by saving rain water. He was picked up at the mouth of the Amazon by a Brazilian fisherman. Two weeks later he set out for Britain, where he asked the Ben Line for another ship.

Mediterranean ports, South and West Africa, the West Indies and the Far East were but a few of the places served by shipping using these docks.

In the Millwall Docks, ships served another mixed bag of oversea ports. The Swedish Lloyd steamers, linking the Thames with Scandinavia, were particularly immaculate, even white-enamelling their anchors. The house flag of the Strick Line, serving the Red Sea and Persian Gulf, incorporated part of the town arms of Swansea, where the line was first established. Elder Dempster, based on Liverpool, ran a subsidiary West Coast of Africa service from the Millwall Docks.

The Royal Docks were the home of those two immortal ships, the *Rawalpindi*, already mentioned in connection with the Children's Beach, and the *Jervis Bay*, which deliberately sacrificed herself to save the convoy she was guarding. The *Rawalpindi* was part of the P&O line. This famous company was begun in 1837 by Arthur Anderson, the son of a poor Shetland fisherman, a junior partner in the firm of Wilcox and Anderson. The firm was broker and agent for a small fleet of insignificant sailing ships trading to Spain and Portugal. Beside good Scottish commercial instincts, there must have been a Ruritanian streak in Anderson, for during unsuccessful insurrections in those two countries he intrigued in Throgmorton Street on behalf of Spanish and Portuguese monarchies. He became *persona grata* at both courts and gained valuable commercial concessions. As a result, the firm began to send a fleet of small paddle steamers to both countries.

In 1840 Anderson added the "O"—Oriental—to his Peninsular Steam Company by obtaining a Royal Charter, on the understanding that the service would be extended to India within two years. India via the Cape was beset with bunkering problems and Anderson turned his attention to the existing Overland Route. The route ran from Alexandria to the Red Sea, both ends connecting with ships. It was always an adventurous journey and sometimes hazardous. Travellers had to carry their own drinking water, washing was forbidden and the ravenous vermin which infested the barges and coaches were among the least of their troubles.

Anderson now built big new steamers for the service to Alexandria, river steamers were sent out to Egypt, hotels were built, distilling plant was installed, and new ships met the travellers at the Red Sea end. Most of the company's problems disappeared when the Suez Canal was opened in 1869. The P&O house flag commemorates something of the company's history, for it combines the blue and white of the Portuguese royal colours and the red and yellow of the Spanish ensign. Seamen were taught the right way to bend on the flag with the jingle: "Blue to the mast, red to the fly, yellow to the deck and white to the sky."

The *Jervis Bay* belonged to the Aberdeen and Commonwealth Line. These ships with their fine lines and green hulls were lineal descendants of the old Aberdeen tea and wool clippers. Nearby berthed the ships of the Port Line, both companies engaged in the Australian trade. Meat and dairy produce from New Zealand for London was carried by a number of lines. Prominent was the New Zealand Shipping Company, originally founded to encourage a

The P&O armed merchant cruiser Rawalpindi, sunk with heavy loss of life on 3rd November, 1939, defending a convoy against two German battleships.
Courtesy: Museum in Dockland

The Aberdeen and Commonwealth Line Jervis Bay *in action to save a convoy from a German battleship. She went down with colours still flying.*
Courtesy: Museum in Dockland

good class of settler. Up to the outbreak of war, the company had a magnificent fleet of passenger and cargo liners, all bearing Maori names. The queens of the fleet were the three lovely sisters, *Rangitata*, *Rangitiki* and the ill-fated *Rangitane*, whose survivors were marooned by the enemy on the lonely beach of Emirau.

Another company berthing in the Royal Docks and serving New Zealand was Shaw, Savill and Albion; one ship, the *Dominion Monarch*, went via the Cape, the other ships through the Panama Canal. This company's house flag was once the national flag of New Zealand. A meeting of Maori chiefs and settlers was held at the Bay of Islands in 1834 to select a national flag. A design consisting of St George's Cross, and with a similar cross and four six-pointed stars on a blue field in the upper hoist, was selected from three designs. This remained the New Zealand national ensign until it was superseded by the Union Flag when the islands were ceded to Queen Victoria under the Treaty of Waitangi in 1840.

Yet more Royal Docks ships trading to New Zealand were owned by the Federal Line. This company, it will be remembered, flew the house flag of Money Wigram, who, as we have seen, quarrelled with Richard Green more than a hundred years ago.

South America was equally well served from these docks. Although vessels of the Blue Star Line went to North Pacific Coast ports, the Cape, Australia and New Zealand, its main trade was in South American chilled beef and green fruit. The "Artists" of Lamport and Holt, the "Granges" of Houlder Bros, and the "Highlands" of Royal Mail Lines were all engaged in this important meat trade.

The principal line among Royal Docks ships serving the African coasts was the Union Castle company. Started in 1900 in the flag-waving atmosphere of the Boer War by the amalgamation of the old-established Union and Castle Lines, the intermediate vessels served the Cape, East and South-west Africa. A traditional feature was the playing of the National Anthem by the ship's orchestra when outward bound from Tilbury Passenger Stage.

Other ships trading to and from African ports were the "Cities" of Ellerman lines, passenger and cargo liners of The British India Company, and the Mauritian sugar ships of T. and J. Harrison, the last of the big steamship companies to be privately owned.

The P&O was not the only line serving India and Burma from the Royal Docks. Brocklebank's Well Line was distinguished by wearing its house flag at the foremast instead of, as customary, the mainmast. In earlier days, this company's windships were under charter to the Honourable East India Company. That autocratic body, it is alleged, insisted on its own flag flying from the mainmast. The company, however, inclined to the theory that the flag, first worn by their ships in 1820, was originally hoisted at the foremast because most of their brigs (two masts) were armed under Letters of Marque and so flew a pennant at the mainmast.

The P&O was found at Malayan ports as well as the Glen Line. Royal Docks vessels bound for the Far East were (once again) P&O, Holt's Blue Funnel Line and (before the war) the Nippon Yusen Kaisha. The Blue Funnel ships all bore the classical names from Greek mythology. As might be expected, the names were usually pronounced in weird and humorous fashion by dockside workers. *Themistocles*, of course, became *Themistockles* ("*as cockles*"). And when an inquirer asked a dock policeman where the urinal was, the reply was: "Blue Funnel? End of the dock." The Nippon Yusen Kaisha brought cargoes of exotic Japanese foodstuffs not then familiar to insular diners. Even HM Customs were sometimes puzzled and demanded a list of ingredients. I remember one Japanese business man endorsing his Bill of Lading with: "I do declare this good was unsweeting".

The principal Royal Docks line serving Canada and the United States was the Cunard White Star. Their *Georgic* and *Britannic*, each some 27,000 gross tonnage, were, before the war, the world's largest motor ships. As we saw in an earlier chapter, the Royal Docks only once berthed the Cunarder *Mauretania*, of some 36,000 gross tonnage, then the largest vessel to use the Port of London (small fry in comparison with today's tonnages!). Serving US ports were ships of the American Merchant Line, which, seemed to have the loudest steam whistles. Other ships using the Royal Docks served Iceland, the Canaries and Mediterranean ports.

185

We have seen the little sea waifs that brought softwood timber to the Surrey Commercial Docks, but more notable ships also berthed there, particularly in the Greenland Dock. Small "A" class (*Ausonia*, *Alaunia*) Cunarders and the "Beavers" of Canadian Pacific brought Canadian dairy produce to refrigerated warehouses (blitzed during the war) to these docks.

Vessels of the Cunard White Star fleet used to wear the house flags of both companies up to the war. The late Boyd Cable, one of the authorities on house flags, offered convincing evidence that the Cunard flag is linked with the Honourable East India Company. The design is of a rampant lion wearing an imperial crown and bearing in its paws a globe showing the western hemisphere, all in yellow on a red field. The flag resembles the crest of the Honourable Company and that of its cadet college at Haileybury. And when Samuel Cunard was seeking backing for his projected steam line, the Honourable Company introduced him to George Burns, a Glasgow shipowner. Thus the present Cunard flag probably symbolizes a "Thank you" to the Honourable East India Company.

The White Star house flag, a red swallow-tail bearing a large white five-pointed star, was the original flag of Pilkington and Wilson. The reputation of their clipper ships was so high that when the line was sold in 1867 T. H. Ismay paid £1,000 for the flag and name.

The Canadian Pacific Line was founded by the Canadian Pacific Railway Company with the object of encouraging good-class British settlers to emigrate to Canada and develop the new lands opened up by the iron road. Furness Withy, also berthing in the Surrey Docks, served the Pacific coast of Canada.

One of the most interesting house flags of ships berthing in these docks was that of the Henderson Line. It was a French tricolour reversed, with a small Union Flag superimposed. Permission to adopt the tricolour as house flag was given to the company by the French Government in return for services rendered during the Crimean War. But the colours were later reversed to avoid confusion of nationality.

The two principal companies using Tilbury Docks before containers swept the board were, once again, the P&O and the Orient Line. Both served intermediate ports on their route to Australasia. Some of the P&O liners, formerly on that run, are now popular cruise ships, based on Southampton. I was lucky enough to be a guest of the P&O on a number of shake-down cruises with new ships. In the *Canberra* I once had a lesson in practical navigation. A fellow passenger, on the second day out, asked me where we were. Without charts or sextant, I hedged. "Well, I'm only a landlubber", said my companion. "But I'll soon tell you where we are." And he went to a deck telephone booth and 'phoned the ship's bridge, returning, looking smug, with the information.

I remember the mighty voices of P&O ships booming out a welcome to the Royal Yacht *Britannia*, bearing the Queen home at the end of her Commonwealth Tour in 1954. As the yacht passed Tilbury Docks where they were berthed, the liners, together with all the other ships in dock, gave the customary "Cock-a-doodle-doo" on their whistles. And I was much amused to hear it answered in tiny falsetto by a small steam crane on the Gravesend side.

The Orient Line vessels (absorbed by the P&O after the war) were descended from that small Rotherhithe fleet of Bilbe, already mentioned. These ships, like those of the P&O, were limited in size by the Suez Canal to about 22,000 gross tonnage. In common with most progressive lines, these ships, when they returned after a round voyage, were thoroughly fumigated with prussic acid gas, which is death to stowaway vermin of all kinds. But it would have also meant death to any humans foolish enough to have boarded the ships during the process. So, while fumigation was taking place, Orient Line vessels flew a warning flag consisting of a black skull and cross-bones on a black-bordered yellow field: in other words, the Jolly Roger of the pirates.

Teak was a prominent cargo in Bibby Line ships at Tilbury Docks, and their holds were designed for the stowage of huge baulks of that hardwood from Rangoon. Up to a few years before the war, Bibby Line ships wore a plain red house flag. But red flags were not popular in some of the ports at which the ships called, so the company tactfully decided to avoid political misconception by superimposing the crest of the Bibby family in gold on the old flag. Several other shipping lines also used Tilbury Docks, and some old-style break-bulk vessels still berth there. But the greatly enlarged docks are now mainly occupied with containers, packaged timber and other modern marine cargo.

On our way downstream we looked briefly at some of the windships and other vessels of character. Of vessels berthing in the river, one we now meet was *John Williams VI*, which I saw in the Pool in 1948. When Princess Margaret named this new motor ship of the London Missionary Society she was aiding the continuity of a remarkable seafaring tradition.

In 1798 the Society began its campaign to evangelize the Pacific Islands by sending from Blackwall the little *Duff* of only 300 gross tonnage. Up to a decade ago, then, it had a missionary and school ship in those parts. Inspired by the good work done by the *Duff*, John Williams, a London apprentice, took up mission work in 1817 at Raratonga. In order to carry the Gospel to outlying groups, he and his devoted islanders built a makeshift vessel, the *Messenger of Peace*. His success was such that he was eventually presented with a new ship, the *Camden*, in which he left the Thames in 1838. A year later he was killed trying to convert some particularly degraded cannibals.

His death started a noteworthy movement. Children in Great Britain, Australia, New Zealand, Canada and South Africa began collecting small sums to perpetuate the memory of the missionary. This money was used by the Missionary Society to build the first *John Williams*, a barque. Every five years she returned to the Thames to refit. Thousands of children inspected her and collected thousands of pounds to keep her sailing. She was eventually lost in 1861.

The second *John Williams* was also a barque and was lost. The third barque of the same name sailed the South Seas for twenty-eight years without mishap. The fourth *John Williams*, a steamship, was superseded in 1930 by an auxiliary schooner, which was replaced by the vessel named by the Princess. This was the only ship registered in London built by the efforts of children in Great Britain and other Commonwealth countries, and she was a staunch and well-known link between the Thames and lovelier rivers overseas. She is believed to have been broken up after the war.

A memorial linking the Thames with two of the Franklin relief expeditions is on the Greenwich waterfront. It commemorates the efforts of Joseph Bellot, a French naval officer and noted Arctic explorer, who in 1851 and again in 1852 joined expeditions seeking to solve the mystery of the lost *Erebus* and *Terror*. No one now seems to know why the memorial was erected at Greenwich.

The modern trade in imported oil virtually began in this country in 1862 when the brig *Elisabeth Watts*, only 224 gross tonnage, arrived in the Thames from Philadelphia with some 1,200 wooden barrels of oil. The cargo was discharged at the Royal Victoria Dock, and the master no doubt breathed a sigh of relief when the last barrel had gone. With so inflammable a cargo, the *Elizabeth Watts* had great difficulty in finding a crew. Eventually she was manned largely by a draft of drunks, shanghaied on the eve of sailing. From that little ship grew the giant tankers which have presented many world ports with the problem of creating ever deeper channels. Tankers of over 200,000 dead weight tonnage have used the Thames in recent years.

Coal is a fuel with a much older lineage than oil. It has already featured from time to time in these notes, and the story of colliers is a great part of the story of the Thames. The story of North Sea colliers, 1939–45, is part of the story of London at war*.

Regarded in marine circles through the centuries as something of a poor relation, the collier nevertheless played a vital role in the growth of our merchant navy, in the development of warships and in the birth of the Industrial Revolution. Until then, the traffic principally served the City's domestic needs; lime burning seems to have been the only Thames-side industry which then consumed coal. Even so, imported coal was taxed in the fourteenth century to provide for the upkeep of London Bridge. And it continued to be bled for objectives as unrelated to coal as the rebuilding of London after the Great Fire (the instigator of that levy must have had a warm sense of humour), the reconstruction of some London churches, the endowment of orphanages, etc.

In more lawless days the east coast collier was the prey of pirates, and everytime we engaged in a war with a Continental country, the colliers were attacked by raiders. And all the time, the little colliers of the sail endured the turbulence of one of the world's worse seas along a then ill-lighted coast with all too few harbours for shelter.

To add to the difficulties of collier crews, a type of ship evolved in which capacity became all important, and the resultant box-like, unhandy, often overloaded vessel taxed the seamanship, endurance and courage of their men to the utmost. As a result, the naval press gangs came to regard these collier fleets as a heaven-sent pool of first-class hands. That the North Sea bred fine seamen is evidenced by the fact that Drake, Nelson, Cook, Conrad, and probably others whose names stand out in our nautical annals, learned much of the rudiments of the sailor's skills along our east coast.

The ships themselves were of all sizes and types, but the most numerous were the famous collier brigs. Manned by large crews to handle their big spread of canvas, they made from eight to ten voyages a year. Incidentally, the charming legend about the fortune made by Dick Whittington is believed to be founded on the type of coasting collier known as a catt.

Most of our east coast rivers were difficult places to leave in the days of sail, and colliers were often held up for long periods by adverse winds at Tyne Bar. Sometimes they were driven by North Sea weather, which must be experienced to be appreciated, to take shelter in the Humber or at Yarmouth or Harwich. If the delay was protracted, the price of coal in the Capital went up like smoke. Then when the wind changed or the weather relented, they would crowd on sail and arrive in the Thames together, sometimes 300

The Thames on Fire by L. M. Bates (Terence Dalton Ltd, 1985)

The arrival of the OCL vessel Encounter Bay, *the first vessel to use the Northfleet Hope riverside container terminal on 15th September, 1968.* Photo: Port of London Authority

strong. Jockeying for position or a mooring, it was not unusual for crews to use violence towards each other and towards the unfortunate officials responsible for regulating berthing. Each ship would then be surrounded by a brood of coal barges, all indifferent to the needs of other vessels requiring room to manoeuvre, and the resultant confusion and congestion were at times chaotic. It was this irregularity and volume of the collier traffic and the harm it did to London's oversea trade that principally led to the building of the enclosed docks, which early in the nineteenth century were the beginning of the Port of London as it is today.

The docks were, however, reserved for the deep-sea ships that had found so much difficulty in discharging and in protecting their cargoes in the congested and often lawless port; the colliers continued to use the river. In early times, long before the era of enclosed docks, the imported coal trade appears to have centred at wharves along the Fleet River, and Seacoal Lane in the vicinity of that former waterway still serves to perpetuate the traffic. It was not long, however, before the trade became too vast for colliers to secure alongside, and overside discharge into barges became customary.

The cargo was discharged by "jumpers", sometimes consisting of shore gangs and sometimes provided by the crew. These jumpers, usually four or five men working as a team, hoisted laden baskets from the hold by jumping off a staging. More than sixty tons were often discharged by this means in a day. The necessity for taking in ballast (and the problem of disposing of it before taking in a fresh cargo) was one of the reasons why the sailing colliers took so long to complete the round voyage.

It is regrettable from the point of view of posterity that our forefathers refused to complicate life by the keeping of detailed records, and figures of London's collier traffic are sketchy and uncertain until near the end of the eighteenth century. We find in 1798 that London imported about 870,000 tons. By the beginning of the end of the sailing collier, in the middle of the nineteenth century, more than ten thousand arrivals carrying a total of nearly four million tons were recorded in one year.

The development of rail communication between the coal fields and London first sketched the doom of the collier windships, for their protracted and irregular voyagings could not compete with the speed and regularity of the coal train; for a time it seemed as if the long and honourable service given to the Capital by the seacoal route would at last come to an end. But in 1852 Charles Palmer put, so to speak, an iron in the fire by building the *John Bowes*, an iron, screw steamship, for the traffic. This vessel carried 650 tons of coal from the Tyne to London in 48 hours. Within a short time the steam collier carried six times as much coal each year as the average sailing collier and made about three times the number of voyages made under sail. Only fifteen years after their introduction the coasting collier trade was carried almost exclusively in steamships. The more orthodox type of vessel evolved still further into the flatiron, the ship with collapsible mast and funnel, able to pass under Thames bridges, which we met during our passage downstream.

Until post-war ocean-trading vessels turned to oil-firing or diesel engines, and riverside gas works and power stations began to decline in number, London imported annually over fifteen million tonnes of coal.

After the war, before the virtual disappearance of seaborne coal from the Thames began, I was privileged to look over the *Hudson River*, a collier, only two years old, then lying at Dagenham. She was a handsome vessel of some three thousand gross register tonnage, of sturdy build but with lines that would not have disgraced a ship in a more colourful trade. All her machinery was aft in order to facilitate loading and discharge.

She carried an average total of 4,200 tonnes in five holds and made some forty-eight round voyages a year. Three such vessels could be accommodated at any one time at Samuel Williams's Dagenham wharf and more than a million tonnes were handled there every year.

The lineal descendants of the old-time jumpers consisted of four huge grabs operated by electric cranes. I watched each grab plunge into the bowels of the *Hudson River* and take four-tonne mouthfuls at one bite. Some of the grabs discharged their coal overside into barges; some dropped their loads into the rail trucks which filed in regulated stops and starts along the jetty. I learnt, incidentally, that the holds usually contained different grades of coal and that there are actually more than thirty kinds in the trade.

Captain Platt, master of the *Hudson River*, took me over his ship in much the same spirit as newly-weds show off their household treasures.

In the crew's quarters, I toured two-berth cabins for all hands, bathrooms, oilskin lockers, soiled-clothes lockers and other features undreamed of by the crews of colliers of only one or two decades before. On the bridge I found the greatest change in this ancient traffic. In addition to the standard fittings this was equipped with Decca navigator, radar, the switchboard for a loud-speaking telephone circuit, echo-sounding gear, loud-hailing apparatus, electrical mechanism for operating the steam whistle, which, in fog, could be set to blow automatically every two minutes as prescribed by regulations, clear-view bridge screens, a radio two-way telephone for communication with the shore and many other navigation aids usually found, in those days, only in deep-sea ships.

In the opinion of Captain Platt, who had had fourteen years' experience of the east coast collier lane, he and his crew were now more comfortable afloat than housing problems permitted them to be ashore, a potential source of worry to wives already rivalled by their husbands' traditional love for their ships.

The master explained that although the conventional run between the Tyne and London was about three hundred miles each way these aids enabled the ship, when conditions were suitable, to take short cuts and so substantially reduce the length of the passage.

It was all very different from what I had read about the old-time collier trade; yet, despite the scientific planning of this ship, I felt that the character of North Sea colliermen had changed little. The sturdy independence of the master, and a subsequent talk with the wharf superintendent emphasized that the feather-bedding of modern conditions had not diminished pride in fast passages under difficult conditions.

I went ashore, happy to feel that the best of the old had been grafted on to the new. On the roof of the company's offices was a slender radio mast, emblematic of the modern world; beside it was a wind vane consisting of a model, old-time Thames spritsail barge. Together, they seemed something of a symbol of this ancient and modern trade.

Alas! Progress has little time for tradition. The Thames trade in seaborne coal has now virtually disappeared and ships like the *Hudson River* and the upstream flatirons have gone with the gasworks and power stations.

One day, if mankind does not destroy the planet, coal, oil and uranium will give out. And unless some new and at present unknown source of energy is discovered, the old skills of sailors of the sail would have to be revived. With few exceptions, the ships of my day were not the ships of today. Nevertheless, despite bigger and better aircraft, despite more trunk roads and tunnels, water continues to provide the cheapest form of transport, and we live, and will long continue to live, by ships.

> I have seen old ships sail like swans asleep
> Beyond the village which men still call Tyre.
> With leaden age o'ercargoed, dipping deep
> For Famagusta and the hidden sun . . .
>
> It was so old a ship—who knows, who knows?
> —And yet so beautiful, I watched in vain
> To see the mast burst open with a rose,
> And the whole deck put on its leaves again.*

*"The Old Ships" by James Elroy Flecker.

192

Selected Bibliography

Bates, L. M. *The Thames on Fire*. Terence Dalton, 1985.

Bird, James. *The Geography of the Port of London*. Hutchinson, 1957.

Broodbank, Sir Joseph G. *History of the Port of London*. 2 vols, O'Connor, 1921.

Carr, R. J. M. (ed.). *Dockland: an Illustrated Historical Survey of Life and Work in East London*. NELP, 1986.

Clegg, Paul W. *Docks and Ports 2. London*. Ian Allen, 1987.

Cohen, Ben. *The Thames 1580–1980: a General Bibliography*. Ben Cohen, 716 Endsleigh Court, London WC1H 0HW, 1985.

Douglas-Brown, R. *The Port of London*. Terence Dalton, 1978.

Linney, A. G. *Lure and Lore of London's River*. Sampson Low, Marston, 1932.

Linney, A. G. *Peepshow of the Port of London*. Sampson Low, Marston, 1930.

Pudney, John. *London's Docks*. Thames and Hudson, 1975.

The former PLA head offices on Tower Hill. Courtesy: Port of London Authority

Index of Illustrations

Index

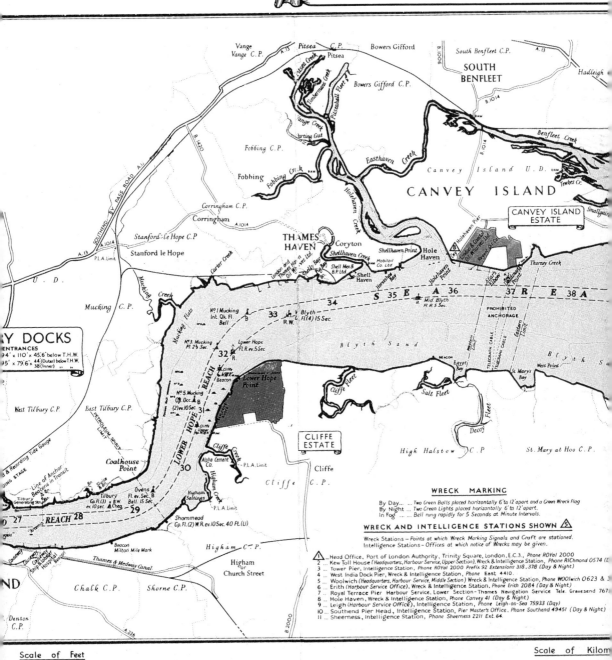

WRECK MARKING

By Day ... Two Green Balls placed horizontally 6' to 12' apart and a Green Wreck Flag
By Night ... Two Green Lights placed horizontally 6' to 12' apart.
In Fog ... Bell rung rapidly for 5 Seconds at Minute Intervals.

WRECK AND INTELLIGENCE STATIONS SHOWN ⚠

Wreck Stations – Points at which Wreck Marking Signals and Craft are stationed.
Intelligence Stations – Offices at which notice of Wrecks may be given.

⚠ ... Head Office, Port of London Authority, Trinity Square, London, E.C.3., Phone ROYal 2000
2 ... Kew Toll House (Headquarters, Harbour Service, Upper Section), Wreck & Intelligence Station, Phone RIchmond 0574 (D
3 ... Tower Pier, Intelligence Station, Phone ROYal 2000 Prefix 92 Extensions 318, 378 (Day & Night)
4 ... West India Dock Pier, Wreck & Intelligence Station, Phone East 4410.
5 ... Woolwich (Headquarters, Harbour Service, Middle Section) Wreck & Intelligence Station, Phone WOOlwich 0623 & 3
6 ... Erith (Harbour Service Office), Wreck & Intelligence Station, Phone Erith 2084 (Day & Night)
7 ... Royal Terrace Pier Harbour Service, Lower Section - Thames Navigation Service Tele. Gravesend 767
8 ... Hole Haven, Wreck & Intelligence Station, Phone Canvey 41 (Day & Night)
9 ... Leigh (Harbour Service Office), Intelligence Station, Phone Leigh-on-Sea 75933 (Day)
10 ... Southend Pier Head, Intelligence Station, Pier Master's Office, Phone Southend 49451 (Day & Night)
11 ... Sheerness, Intelligence Station, Phone Sheerness 2211 Ext. 64.

Scale of Feet

15000   20000   25000   30000 FEET

METRES 1000 500. 0   1   2   3   4   5

Scale of Kilo